What FACULTY are saying about . . .

Success

in MIDDLE SCHOOL
A TRANSITION ROAD MAP

"Finally, a resource that speaks to and for middle school students. I wished I had this as I was planning my transition program—I would have used it throughout the program and would have given some away as prizes. However, it doesn't stop there, *Success in Middle School* extends itself to be a great resource for all educators as they work with transition programs in their schools."

Davina R. Johnson
SCHOOL COUNSELING DIRECTOR, JOHN ROLFE MIDDLE SCHOOL, RICHMOND, VA

"*Success in Middle School* will best be used as an interactive tool for soon-to-be middle school students. The book offers many important points that can help students make a successful social and emotional transition from elementary to middle school."

Sharlita Ramirez
DIRECTOR OF STUDENT PROGRAMS/DEAN OF STUDENTS, BREAKTHROUGH KENT DENVER

"Middle school students face enormous challenges, both academically as they prepare to enter a global economy, and emotionally because they're growing up and entering adulthood. In our quest as educators to help them become a better student and citizen, this book can help prepare students for what lies ahead."

Steve Chavis
SPECIAL NEEDS AIDE, PULASKI FINE ARTS ACADEMY, CHICAGO

"There is important and valuable information in this book that students won't get on their own. It lays a solid foundation for a successful transition from elementary school to middle school."

Joanne Slingerland
CURRICULUM COORDINATOR FOR CENTRAL WYOMING COLLEGE, GEAR UP

"The writing is to the point and easy to understand for teens, and the *'Thinking to Myself'* sections are great. Terms were clearly defined and easy to access.

Devin Dillon
PRINCIPAL, GREENWOOD K-8; DENVER, COLORADO

"I love the vocabulary and definitions! The text is engaging and interactive. It's a truly great resource."

Lori Ebanietti
7TH GRADE TEACHER, EISENHOWER MIDDLE SCHOOL, COLORADO

"*Success in Middle School* engages the reader with narratives that show the inner thinking of a real middle school student. Students will treasure this book because it shows them they are not alone in their concerns about middle school."

Grace White
6TH GRADE LANGUAGE ARTS TEACHER AT EISENHOWER MIDDLE SCHOOL, COLORADO

"This will be a helpful resource in the transition to middle school. There are topics addressed that parents may not think of talking to their children about."

Kim Cobb, LPC
COUNSELOR (7TH GRADE AND 8TH GRADE) EVERGREEN MIDDLE SCHOOL

"It is the only comprehensive middle school tool that I'm aware of, and it's wonderful. *Success in Middle School* offers a helpful way to talk about and address the multiple issues students face."

Jennifer Baker
COUNSELOR, DUNSTAN MIDDLE SCHOOL, LAKEWOOD, CO

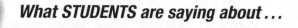

Success

in MIDDLE SCHOOL
A TRANSITION ROAD MAP

"You face a lot of changes when you start middle school, and this book can help you know how to deal with them."

Justin Jenkins, *high school student, Nashville, TN*

"I would have liked reading this book last year to help me overcome my failing grade in math during the first quarter. I KNOW some students in 6th grade struggle with bad grades, and this book can really help them with their grades and other issues like belonging."

Julie Hardy, *7th grader, Colorado Springs, CO*

"I'm going into middle school, and this book definitely gave me some good advice. In every chapter, they give examples of problems a middle school student might face. These stories allow students to use their imagination to solve the dilemmas."

Maggie Mehlman, *5th grade, Denver, CO*

"I like the cartoon bubbles because these are situations that happen in real life, and they help you think about what the chapter is really about."

Ian Carter, *6th grade, Bethesda, MD*

"*Success in Middle School* helps students be prepared for what is ahead in the future."

Sarah Graff, *5th grade, Denver, CO*

"I really like this book because it helps you see middle school as one big adventure. Also, there are some interesting stories about real kids that you can relate to."

"I would have appreciated reading a book like this in middle school because when I was a student no one really addressed puberty or taking care of your brain. I also like the book's idea of picking classes and extracurricular activities as preparation for the future."

"I think the value of this book lies in teaching kids to embrace their own strengths, not those that society assigns value to (such as being a star quarterback, cheerleader, etc.). Just because queen bees might be popular doesn't make them good role models. This book also talks about cyber bullying, which is a big issue for many students."

Success

in MIDDLE SCHOOL

A TRANSITION ROAD MAP

Carol Carter

LifeBound
DENVER, COLORADO

President/Publisher: Carol J. Carter—LifeBound, LLC
Editorial Director/Contributor: Cynthia Nordberg
Developmental Editor: Maureen Breeze
Managing Editor: Sara Fuller
Assistant Editors: Amy Piazza, Kristen Fenwick, Heather Brown
Cover & Interior Design: John Wincek
Contributing Photographers: Alyssa Groleau

LifeBound, LLC
1530 High Street
Denver, CO 80218
Tel. 1.877.737.8510
www.lifebound.com

Dedication

To Ed Stanford, who has believed in kids of all
ages through his dedication to public education
and, to the "child" within himself who will always
be supportive, curious and open to learning no
matter how old he may be.

Contents

Preface

Success in Middle School is designed to help you make the most of the next few years. We hope it inspires you to prepare for the many changes ahead. In addition to the primary text, each chapter contains the following elements.

First, every chapter includes situational narratives placed inside cartoon bubbles. These stories explore a variety of middle school students' experiences. You won't relate to all of them, but read them with the knowledge that some of your peers might be experiencing some of the situations. Many of the narratives describe dilemmas that don't necessarily have a right or wrong answer. Try to imagine what you would do if you were in these situations. They offer a great opportunity to learn from others.

Second, every chapter contains a series of vocabulary words that appear in bold within the text. You'll find their definitions next to the acronym **W2R** (words to remember). These words will appear again at the end of the chapter. Although you may already be familiar with several of them, stretch yourself when you're asked to use the words in a sentence at the end of each chapter. Write in terms of how these words apply to your life.

Third, each chapter contains profile stories written by middle and high school students from across the country. Unlike the situational narratives, these stories are unique and are included to emphasize the fact that success is possible for every middle school student, especially in the wake of challenge and failure.

Fourth, each chapter contains an *Asking Questions! Reflect and Respond* section. Take time to thoughtfully answer the questions. They are designed to help you think about your life in terms of where you are now and where you hope to go in the future.

Acknowledgments

s students move from elementary to middle school they encounter a significant transition of academic, emotional and social challenges. Our goal for *Success in Middle School* has been to set a new standard on preparedness for these transitory years, an objective that's made possible by the feedback and insights from our diverse team of reviewers. I would like to acknowledge the following people who contributed significantly to this project:

Administrators, Counselors, Librarians, and Teachers, who shared their expertise in helping us shape the content: Tammy Bagdely, Jennifer Baker, Steve Chavis, Kim Cobb, Devin Dillon, Lori Ebanietti, Nate Howard, Kate Moore, Donna Sanders, Kathleen Scheppe, Grace E. White, Joanne Slingerland, Mary Whitman, and Christa Holm.

Parent Reviewers, who gave their heartfelt input as champions of their children: Carol Garcia, Kate Moore, Sue O'Neil, Cheryl Turner, and Tim Nordberg.

Our robust group of elementary and middle school students, who helped us field test the book before it went to print: Ian Carter, Luke Dowdy, Sarah Graff, Julie Hardy, Maggie Mehlman, Mackenzie Moore, and Trent Nordberg.

Our current and former LifeBound interns, who offered their unique perspectives as college students and recent graduates: Brianna Boeschenstein, Brande Micheau, Heather Brown, Laura Daugherty, Amy Piazza, and Brittany Zachritz.

Our talented photographer, Alyssa Groleau, who provided most of the opening chapter photos; and to our cadre of friends, whose pictures enhanced the text throughout the book: Sarah and Emily Armstrong, Maureen Breeze, Wyatt and Sawyer Goddard, Kate Moore, MacKenzie Moore, and Rosemary Wolff.

Our editorial team: Maureen Breeze for her diligent and insightful work on the manuscript; our managing editor Cynthia Nordberg, who contributed the student profile stories and kept the project on task; and Sara Fuller, Conor McKenzie, Diane Knight, and Jim Hoops for helping us with the review process.

I'm grateful for the role each of you have played in creating a resource that optimally prepares elementary school students for the challenges ahead.

All the best,

Carol Carter

AUTHOR AND PRESIDENT
LifeBound

About the Author

arol Carter is a national and international transition expert. She has written or co-authored over 25 books on school, college, career and life success and has been a host in over 40 countries in her travels around the globe. The photograph on the back cover of this book is of Carol's visit to Morocco. Her books have been translated into Chinese and Spanish. Her series, *The Keys to Success* is used widely in the first year of college and has been read by over **one million students** since it was published. For more information on Carol's college books,

visit **www.carterkeys.com**. You can also see the front cover of these titles in the back of this book on the page, "Other Books by Carol Carter."

Carol's company, LifeBound, specializes in **success and transition** programs for students in the fifth through twelfth grades. LifeBound produces books, curricula and training programs for schools across the country focusing on freshmen academies, small learning communities, and other models of innovation to help every child achieve their potential. In addition,

LifeBound teaches adult learners in the housing projects, and has worked with inmates in the Federal prison system. These experiences indicate what is lacking for some students when they go through public education, and what is possible for all students if they value and respect themselves and others, if they work hard to maximize their strengths and improve their weaknesses, and if they develop a vision for themselves and their future that is honorable, courageous and bold.

LifeBound also trains and certifies faculty, school executives and professors in the skills of **academic coaching.** All of learning is based on emotion and coaching helps develop a variety of skills including asking powerful questions. When students learn to answer these questions for themselves, they are challenged, motivated and engaged as lifelong learners. LifeBound sessions are held in the Denver offices several times throughout the year, and Carol and her leadership team go to colleges and districts to train staff on coaching skills on location. For more information, please visit www.lifebound.com and Carol's blog is www.caroljcarter.com.

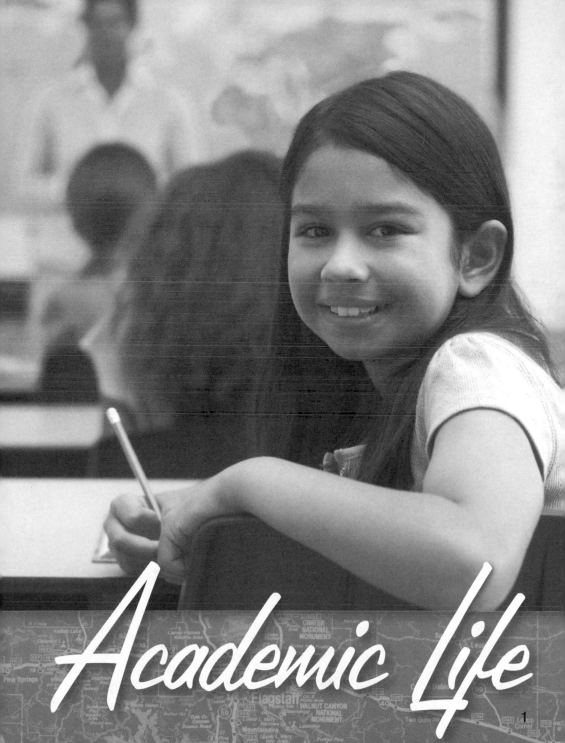

PART I

Academic Life

Middle School vs. Grade School

WHAT'S DIFFERENT?

s I step off the bus onto the cement pathway that leads up to my new middle school, time seems to freeze. All around me other students scramble inside, talking and laughing as if it were an ordinary day. It isn't just another day—it's my first day of middle school. I'd heard it would be different from grade school, but it

3

didn't sink in until this moment. As I stand before the building I sense change. I miss the comforts of Ms. Halstead's elementary school classroom, but at the same time I'm ready to face new and exciting challenges. I join the crowd of unfamiliar faces, many of them belonging to older students, and head toward the school's entrance. "Hey Michael, over here!" a familiar voice rings out. It's Malcolm, another student who was in Ms. Halstead's class last year. "Maybe this won't be so scary after all," I think as we meet up. Taking a deep breath, I push open the glass door and walk into my new world.

How is middle school different from grade school? Like Michael, you might be filled with mixed emotions. You can't be exactly sure of what's coming, but you know there will be changes. Some of the challenges you'll face include meeting new people and shouldering more responsibilities. Luckily, your experience doesn't need to be a frightening one. With a little preparation, you can navigate your new environment with ease.

This book offers you a road map for the challenges you'll face in middle school. If you haven't started your year yet, this will be a great way for you to prepare. If you've already begun middle school, this book can help you make sense of what's happened so far and help you plan for the months ahead.

More Movement

Michael missed the comforts of Ms. Halstead's class. He liked staying in the same classroom for much of the day and having one person teach all of his core subjects. Your grade school probably followed a similar format. When you moved to other classrooms, as you might have for art and gym class, you were escorted in a single file line with the rest of your peers. In middle school, however, individual interests and abilities begin to surface. Everyone's classes are scheduled according to these differences and you don't have the same exact schedule as other students. And just as you have classes that reflect these special interests, your teachers have specific capabilities and education in the subjects they teach. As a result, classes such as math, science, and English are usually taught by different instructors in various parts of the building. Because each teacher has his or her own classroom, you move independently through the hallways a great deal more than you might have in elementary school.

Thinking to Myself

When I started middle school, I loved all of my new teachers except one. This man terrified me. He was really strict about tardiness and gave a ton of homework. The class was much harder than any I'd ever taken. After a while, I realized he had a pretty good sense of humor and I was learning a lot. I found myself interested in a subject that I'd never cared for. By the end of the year he was my favorite teacher. I'm still trying to figure out how that happened.

1. Why do you think this student might not have liked this teacher at first?

2. What do you think happened that shifted this student's perspective?

Don't be intimidated by using your locker. This is a great place to store your books and organize your personal items.

How you manage your time in between each period is your decision. Whether you need to stop at the bathroom or make a trip to your locker, you're still expected to be in your seat before the next bell rings. You're also expected to show up with the correct books and materials for each course. If this year is your first with a locker, it may take some time for you to figure out how to juggle the number of times you need to use it each day. You need to consider how many minutes you have for each passing period and where your locker is located in relation to each of your classes. Don't worry if you have to write your locker combination on the back of your hand for the first week. You won't be alone.

More Freedom

As you can see, these changes give you more freedom during your day. Just as your class schedule reflects some of your personal interests, you can choose extracurricular activities based on what you like as well. You can join the jazz band, the science club, or even take up Tae Kwon Do with some of the new people you meet.

However, with greater freedom, both in and after school, comes more responsibility. When you are old enough to earn money through baby-sitting, for example, you become **accountable** for the welfare of the children you watch. Similarly, in school you are now **accountable** for getting to class on time, completing assignments for all your courses, and managing your day without one teacher overseeing your schedule. Have fun as the restrictions on you begin to loosen, but you'll be more successful if you take these newfound privileges seriously. Balancing these freedoms and responsibilities is critical, and middle school is the perfect place to develop this ability.

Accountable *responsible to someone or for some action*

ACTIVITY

Read through the list on the following page. What specific responsibilities would be involved if you pursued these goals?

For example, think about serving as your student body president. You might determine that your responsibilities include being a role model, keeping up your grades, planning and executing activities for the student body, and developing strong relationships with your peers and faculty. By not following through with the responsibilities required you might be dismissed from the role, or lose your effectiveness in the position.

1. Getting a job at the shopping mall
2. Having a paper route
3. Organizing an event to raise money for a local homeless shelter
4. Driving a car
5. Traveling to another country
6. Serving as your school president

What conclusions did you draw?

_____

_____

_____

Less Certainty

If you're worried that you won't be up for the challenges of middle school, consider that your peers might be feeling the same way you are: scared, uncertain, and perhaps insecure. Maybe you worry that others will notice your flaws, or that you won't be as smart, pretty, or hip as the other students. It's natural to be unsure of yourself when you move into unknown territory, especially if you were comfortable with the way your life was before. However, try to keep in mind that everyone is going through this transition and that growing up requires moving into new situations. And while being aware of your flaws is a necessary part of developing self-awareness, dwelling too much on what you perceive to be your weaknesses might hold you back as you try to make new friends.

Do you ever look at someone else and wish you were more like him or her? What is it about this person that appeals to you? Often what you are picking up on is their self confidence. Nothing causes people to **gravitate** toward others quite like self confidence. Middle school

Gravitate *to be drawn or pulled in as if by some force*

Backpack tip: Don't carry too much in book weight. Only take home what you need to study.

Seeing Myself in Others

My name is Josh. Now that I'm in middle school I have more choices to make. I play volleyball in the fall, basketball in the winter, and track and baseball in the spring and summer. There are a lot of sports I love to play, but there isn't enough time in the day to play them all. So I've had to make the choice to limit myself.

I'll also have to make decisions about my health that I didn't have to make in grade school. I've had diabetes since I was 5, and managing it will be a bigger responsibility. My diabetes isn't that hard to deal with in general unless I want to eat sweets—which I can't do that often. If I eat a treat that a classmate brings in for his or her birthday, I need to

take more insulin. I calculate my own insulin dosage and am able to take care of myself using an insulin pump, which I keep in my pocket. The pump injects insulin through a tiny needle into my stomach.

Now that I'm in middle school, I have to plan my time carefully in between classes so I can monitor my blood sugar and take insulin when I need to while still getting to my locker and my next class on time. Checking my blood sugar levels every two to three hours a day is the hardest thing I have to remember to do, and it gets to be a hassle. Changing the position of my pump every three days is also a lot of work, but I've learned how to take care of my diabetes well enough to have a normal life.

Diabetes is a part of my life and I'll have it forever, but it's not what defines me. I won't let it become my label. There is much more to who I am. I recently realized that there are a lot of other diseases and illnesses out there that are much worse. My advice to others is this: whether you have diabetes or not, you can live a better life if you make smart choices and get the most out of every situation.

provides infinite opportunities to explore and refine this attribute. Knowing what you are good at, while making efforts to improve on your weaknesses, will help you develop the ability to shine.

Thinking to Myself

Yesterday was my first day of middle school. It went well enough, but as I was getting off the bus at the end of the day I tripped on the last step and fell hands first onto the pavement. My bus stop is at the beginning of the route, so the bus was full of all the neighborhood kids. I'm new to the area and have no friends who ride my bus. I felt humiliated as the younger kids sitting up front laughed. The driver only made it worse by reprimanding them and then rising from her chair to help me. I'll probably spend the rest of middle school being known as the kid who fell off the bus.

1. How do you think this student should handle his next day at school?

2. If you were a neighborhood student on the bus, what could you do to make this boy feel more comfortable?

Greater Complexity

avigating middle school can be complicated. Moving from class to class, balancing the demands of several teachers, and being responsible for managing more of your time poses day to day challenges. Middle school also comes with the **inevitable** demands of social pressure, increased amounts of homework, and the onset of puberty—all of which can be very stressful. Dealing with these complex demands may require a lot of energy and attention. However experiencing changes of this magnitude is an **integral** step toward **maturity**. If these changes begin to overwhelm you, reach out for support. Learning to ask for help and advocate for yourself is one of the most important lessons you can learn. Don't forget that your parents, friends, teachers and school counselors can be allies during this significant period in your life.

Inevitable *unavoidable; without possibility of escape*

Integral *essential or necessary for completeness*

Maturity *full development; adulthood*

vocabulary

Define *accountable*.

_____

_____

_____

_____

Write a sentence about your own life using the word accountable.

_____

_____

_____

Define *gravitate.*

_____

_____

_____

Write a sentence about your own life using the word gravitate.

_____

_____

_____

Define *inevitable.*

_____

_____

_____

Write a sentence about your own life using the word inevitable.

_____

_____

_____

Define *integral*.

_____

_____

_____

Write a sentence about your own life using the word integral.

_____

_____

_____

Define *maturity*.

_____

_____

_____

Write a sentence about your own life using the word maturity.

_____

_____

_____

asking questions

What expectations do you have for yourself as you begin or continue middle school?

_____

_____

_____

_____

_____

What must you do to live up to these expectations?

_____

_____

_____

_____

_____

What excites you about starting middle school? If you've already started, how did you adjust to the differences you found between middle school and grade school?

_____

_____

_____

_____

_____

What does this make you think of?
Journal about your thoughts.

Learning to Learn

HOW CAN YOU STUDY BEST?

oices on the radio pull me from my dream. My alarm's signaling that the dreaded 6:30 a.m. has arrived. I bury myself
under the covers and groan, but the sun peeking through my
curtains tells me I can't delay the inevitable much longer. It's time to
get up and get ready for school—again. "Honey, you're going to be

late!" my mother shouts from downstairs. I toss off my blankets, drag myself out of bed, brush my teeth, and grab the first T-shirt and pair of pants within reach. Who knows if they're clean? I grab two donuts off the counter and shove them down as my mom drives me to school. I wish I had some milk. I arrive with my eyes still half-closed. I'm late, again, so I hurry to my first period and take a seat. Within fifteen minutes I'm dozing off, just like most mornings. I promise myself I'll get to bed before 10:30 tonight, but I know it probably won't happen.

In many parts of the world it is a privilege to go to school. People from these countries have gone to war and risked their lives for an education for themselves and their children. Yet you may have days when you feel like it's an obligation; one more thing that's forced upon you. It can be challenging at times to perceive school as the gift that it is. And yet your attitude can make all the difference in your success. As you mature and take on more responsibility for your future, it is important to ask how you can position yourself to get the most out of school. How can you do your best to receive an education that will open doors and create opportunities for you?

This chapter offers ideas on how you can enhance your study habits both in and out of the classroom. It will cover how you can improve your focus, how you can become more organized, and how to manage your time more effectively. You can be a high achiever in school if you're willing to **capitalize** on your school-related strengths and work to improve your school-related weaknesses. Take a moment to identify your strengths and weaknesses. Keep them in mind as you read through the following sections to see how you can improve your classroom performance.

Capitalize *to profit by*

Thinking to Myself

The closer it gets to lunch time, the more my mind starts to wander. I don't feel like I'm learning anything in my history class, which happens to be right before lunch. Every tap of the pen and scrape of the chair causes me to lose my focus. By the time the bell rings and I pack up to leave, I've taken pages of notes. But I have no idea what I've written.

1. At what time of day do you tend to have the least amount of focus? At what time do you have the best focus? What could be the reasons for this? What might you be able to do to maximize your focus?

2. Where do you typically sit in the classroom—the front, the back, off to the side? How does your seat placement affect your ability to focus?

Staying Focused

Perhaps focus is your weakness. If you're like the student described in the opening of the chapter, you may be so tired that you have a hard time keeping your eyes open. Or maybe you are simply prone to daydreaming. Are you someone who's easily distracted by shuffling papers, squeaky chairs, whispers from those sitting around you, or noises coming from the hallway?

Sometimes improving your focus is simply a matter of making a greater effort to pay attention to your teacher.

However, there are a few other things you can do to improve in this area.

Breakfast can play a significant role in how well you're able to function in class. Eating two donuts for breakfast will keep you from getting hungry for a while. But know you might be setting yourself up to crash after the sugar rush passes. By 10:00 a.m. you could be struggling to stay awake, simply because you had a less than nutritious breakfast. Try eating some fresh fruit and protein to help energize you and keep your stomach satisfied until lunch. Food fuels your brain and helps you maintain alertness, so make sure your early morning meal provides your body with the energy you need to perform your best in class.

It's generous to share, but be careful not to spread germs when you're fighting a cold.

Thinking to Myself

I knew things weren't going as well as I'd hoped for in my fourth period class, but I didn't expect to see an F on my progress report. I feel sick at the thought of what my parents might say, and even worse when I think of what my punishment might be. I wish this was some kind of mistake. I have no idea how I'll be able to bring my grade back up before the end of the semester.

1. What are some steps this student might take to improve his or her grade?

2. How can you keep from ending up in this type of situation?

Taking Good Notes

One trick to help you stay focused in class is to take notes as your teacher speaks. And unless you're one of the few people who can hear something once and lock it to memory, knowing how to take good notes is an essential skill. Your teachers may give you tips on taking notes to maximize your effectiveness in a particular class. Some of them may even require you to use a certain note-taking technique. But it is still important for you to put some thought into developing a note-taking style that works best for you. Make sure to consider using pictures, diagrams, numerical or alphabetical bullet points, abbreviations, and/or symbols if you find them helpful. Write down details and key points that you can study from later. Try not to get too bogged down with every word your teacher says. Over the next few years you'll have plenty of practice to perfect your own note-taking techniques.

Make time to recopy your notes after class. This process can be a fabulous study tool, especially for mathematics.

sequence *a continuous or connected series*

And remember in math class to always write down every step for solving a problem. Don't leave out steps just because they are familiar to you, understanding the entire **sequence** is critical for mathematical success.

Keeping your notes neat, using plenty of space on your page, writing legibly and highlighting main topics are other strategies to help you develop effective note-taking habits.

Asking Questions

Another thing you can do to further your own education is ask questions. To begin with, you should always ask questions when you don't understand something. Other students will appreciate your questions and teachers certainly want you to speak up when things need to be clarified. If you are intimidated and don't want to ask a question in front of the entire class, approach your teacher after the bell rings.

You can take asking questions a step further. What would it be like if you prepared for each class by formulating three questions related to the topic that you are studying? For example, you are discussing earthquakes in science. What if you came to class and wondered:

1. Do earthquakes happen more frequently during specific temperature ranges?

2. How does ocean life react to earthquakes that occur under the sea?

3. What is the school's policy in the event of an earthquake?

Can you see how coming to class armed with questions that interest you will help you participate in class discussion and keep you focused and interested on the lesson?

Relating Knowledge

*F*inally, one of the best ways to learn is to ask yourself how the information you are covering relates to things you've studied before in the class, topics

Be an active class member. Raise your hand, be curious and ask questions.

you've covered in other classes, or information you've gathered outside of school. This process helps you make connections. Imagine you are reading a book about a soldier who was injured in World War II. Can you make connections to recent history (i.e. injured soldiers returning from Iraq)? What about connections to geography (Was this soldier injured in Europe, Russia, Pearl Harbor? What might the terrain of these places look like?)? Perhaps you can make connections to social studies (Was the soldier involved with the Holocaust?). The more connections you can make to new material, the better your chances will be for understanding and remembering the information.

Keeping Organized

Even the brightest of students run into trouble when they misplace a worksheet or forget to write down the due date of an important assignment. Problems like these can be easily avoided if you keep an orderly

locker and backpack, designate a separate notebook for each subject so your notes and worksheets don't get mixed together, and use a day planner. Using a day planner to keep track of homework assignments, test dates, and extracurricular commitments can help you create order out of chaos and make schoolwork much more manageable. Organizing yourself in this way is extremely important in middle school when you no longer have one teacher who oversees most of your work. Only

TIME	MON	TUE	WED
7:00	Don't forget to take graph paper!		Take in cans for food drive
8:00			
9:00	Permission slip for basketball team tryouts due		
10:00		Science test!	
11:00			History report due
12:00			
1:00			
2:00			
3:00		Work on science project w/ Matt	Work on science project w/ Matt
4:00	Math homework Pgs. 78 & 79	Soccer practice	
5:00			
6:00			
7:00	Study for science test tomorrow		Karate class
8:00			Review vocabulary for test
9:00			
10:00			

you will know if you have a math test and science test on the same day. It's up to you to stay on top of your schedule and plan accordingly.

Keeping the necessary school supplies on hand helps you stay organized as well. Having a pouch in your locker with several pencils, pens, and erasers will save you time, especially when you are late to a class! What else can you do to keep yourself organized?

Managing Your Time

While a day planner can help you manage your time and school work effectively, you still need to consider how you can manage your free time after school and on weekends. How can you participate in the activities that interest you, complete your homework and fulfill your family obligations, all while making sure you have time to spend with friends?

Managing your time outside of school might present another challenge for you. Many students' schedules are **inconsistent**. For example, they might have Tuesdays and Fridays wide open, while Mondays, Wednesdays and Thursdays are packed with soccer practice and piano lessons. Can you write up your weekly schedule?

Inconsistent *lacking in agreement between different parts or elements*

Once you know your schedule, make a list of all your obligations each week including chores, homework, sporting games, etc. Now is the important part—prioritize your commitments. What needs to be accomplished each week, each day? Make a list for each day including the "must do list" and the "can do list." Do you have days where you can work ahead and read extra for the week?

Seeing Myself in Others

My name is Dana. School has always come pretty easily to me, and I usually get straight As. I think the main reason I do well academically is because I'm naturally curious. I recently discovered something I never would have guessed I'd like to do: dissect animals. In science lab we dissected a cat, and I became so engrossed with piecing together how everything worked that I stayed after class to explore the organs.

Being able to connect what I learn in school to the real world has been very important to my academic and personal growth. This year, my family hosted a foreign exchange student from Slovakia. Now I'm in Central Europe visiting her, and I've gotten to meet her family and experience her culture. Her father took me soaring in a glider plane, which was something I'd never done before. Gliders have many of the same parts as regular airplanes, but they have smooth skins so they can slip through the air more easily. It was a thrill to ride in one.

During this trip, I'm also going to visit Poland, Croatia, and the Czech Republic. I plan on touring former concentration camps, so I'll actually get to see all the places I've read about in my history books. I can't wait to learn more about them.

I've had my share of struggles, too, and I've had to adapt and be flexible in order to live up to the standards I've set for myself at school. When I tried out for the cheerleading squad and was picked to be an alternate, I was really disappointed. But my motto is to never give up, and not being picked this year won't stop me from trying out again next year. In the meantime, I'll be free to explore other interests.

If you are busy, look to see when you can compensate for an overloaded schedule. By planning ahead and managing your time wisely, you'll surprise yourself with what you can accomplish each week.

Once you devise a plan for managing your time, you need to commit to it. It helps to determine a **definitive** starting point for your homework. Perhaps you get home from school, have a snack and plan to begin your studies at 4:00. The trick is not delaying the start time.

Definitive *final; conclusive; explicit*

If you do, and don't begin until 5:00, you might be interrupted by dinner or soccer practice. Knowing when you need to get your homework done each day, and sticking to your plan, will help you escape procrastination. Nothing is worse than seeing the clock turn 10:00 and you're just starting your book report that's due in the morning!

Everyone has their own ideas about what constitutes academic success. Whatever your definition is, reaching it is ultimately up to you. The assistance your parents and teachers can offer you only goes so far. While it's important to take advantage of this assistance, learning is ultimately your responsibility. There will be times you'll have to fight for knowledge. Conquering pre-algebra and life science might not come easily. But by figuring out the study methods, homework routines, and note-taking strategies that work best for you, you can excel in middle school.

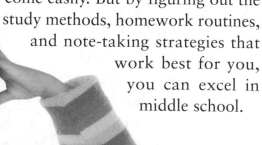

vocabulary

Define *capitalize*.

_____

_____

_____

_____

Write a sentence about your own life using the word capitalize.

_____

_____

_____

_____

Define *sequential*.

_____

_____

_____

_____

Write a sentence about your own life using the word sequential.

_____

_____

_____

_____

Define *inconsistent*.

_____

_____

_____

_____

Write a sentence about your own life using the word
inconsistent.

_____

_____

_____

_____

Define *definitive*.

_____

_____

_____

_____

Write a sentence about your own
life using the word definitive.

_____

_____

_____

_____

_____

_____

asking questions

Do you perform up to your potential in school? Explain.

_____

_____

_____

_____

_____

What actions can you take toward improving your academic performance?

_____

_____

_____

_____

_____

How can you hold yourself accountable for performing your best?

_____

_____

_____

_____

_____

What does this make you think of?
Journal about your thoughts.

PART II

Social Life

Meaningful Friendships

WHAT KIND OF FRIEND ARE YOU AND HOW DO YOU CHOOSE FRIENDS?

I've wanted to talk to Monique ever since I transferred to my new school. We seem to share many interests, and I'm impressed by how kind she is to everyone. During a class discussion she mentioned chess, which is my favorite game to play even though none of my friends ever want to learn. But Monique is in a wheelchair, and I'm afraid she'll think I only want to meet her out of curiosity about her situation. I see her approaching me and start to get nervous. "You're Renee, right?" she asks with a friendly smile. "I noticed you're new. How is everything going so far?" By the end of our conversation, she promises to introduce me at the next chess club meeting. I feel both relieved and excited, and in hindsight I am struck by how strange my initial hesitation was.

How do you form relationships with new people you'd like to have for friends? If going up to strangers and initiating conversation isn't easy for you, don't panic. Worthwhile friendships don't usually develop overnight. Sometimes it takes being in classes together, working on a

Sawyer and Wyatt collect insects and reptiles that are made to resemble the real thing.

joint project, or being a part of a team for relationships to blossom. The group of friends you want to join may not be obvious at first. Finding friends can take time.

Imagine dropping a handful of coins into a jar full of water. The coins—pennies, nickels, dimes, and quarters— have been thrown in at random, somewhat like you and your classmates at your new school. Dropping all the coins into the water creates a bit of chaos. Some veer sideways, and others sink to the bottom. Eventually, each coin settles into its new environment at the jar's base. You and your classmates too will settle into middle school where new friendships will emerge.

Thinking to Myself

I had one best friend throughout elementary school. We had the same teacher every year and spent most afternoons together at one of our houses. Now that all of the smaller elementary schools in our district have fed into one large middle school, we only have one class in common because there are so many more students and teachers. Sometimes I worry about losing her as a best friend, and I don't really want either of us to make too many new friends. I feel a little guilty about my attitude.

1. Why do you think this student doesn't want her best friend to make a lot of new friends?

2. How do you think these best friends can best support each other as they transition into middle school?

Identify Positive Personality Traits

hat do you like about your friends? From the list below, choose the top five attributes that you seek in others. Feel free to include additional characteristics on the lines provided. Go with your first instinct, rather than over thinking the answers:

Fun	Daring	Persevering
Caring	Bold	Compassionate
Quiet	Artistic	Empathetic
Smart	Athletic	Involved
Creative	Organized	Musical
Brainy	Responsible	Adventurous
Silly	Attractive	Honest
Wealthy	Accepting	Humorous
Exciting	Outdoorsy	Successful
Cool	Studious	Peace-Maker
Trustworthy	Respectful	Inquisitive

_____   _____   _____

_____   _____   _____

Attribute *a distinguishing feature that belongs to someone or something*

What do you think attracts you to these qualities? How many of these attributes do you possess? Are you attracted to people who are similar to or different from you?

_____

_____

_____

_____

Now consider qualities that you dislike or avoid in others. Circle your top five choices. Again, add any you wish to include and follow your first instinct:

Boring	Intrusive	Apathetic
Gossipy	Indifferent	Disrespectful
Mean	Cliquish	Irresponsible
Cynical	Aloof	Materialistic
Careless	Negative	Arrogant
Critical	Unpopular	Untrustworthy
Uncaring	Phony	Weak
Selfish	Unattractive	Teacher's pet
Snobby	Judgmental	Trouble-maker
Cold	Intimidating	Unsupportive
Pushy	Uncool	Manipulative

_____   _____   _____

_____   _____   _____

How do you feel when you surround yourself with people who demonstrate these qualities? Do you ever exhibit these traits? Which of these attributes do you want to eliminate from your behavior?

_____

_____

_____

_____

Think about the friends you have and the friendships you want to develop. Are there any changes you'd like to make? What is one specific thing you can do to be a better friend to others?

_____

_____

_____

_____

Discover Mutual Interests

The previous exercise explores how you can identify friends based on personal qualities. Friendships also evolve out of **mutual** interests and activities. A great way to get to know other people is by participating in activities you enjoy doing.

If you like math you might want to consider joining the Math Olympiads team. Or perhaps if you enjoy dancing, what about signing up for the after school hip hop class? By pursuing activities outside of the classroom,

Mutual _held in common between two or more_

you're bound to meet people who share similar interests. And having the opportunity to interact with a smaller number of people may be more beneficial than trying to meet people in your cafeteria or in front of school before the first bell. Being part of a group or close-knit team will help give you a sense of belonging. Middle school seems smaller and more manageable after you've created a community of friends.

ACTIVITY

After-school clubs and extra-curricular activities are great places to build a network of friends. They're also great places to develop and expand your own interests and passions. Below is a list of activities. Circle the ones that interest you:

Dance	Basketball	Drama
Football	Math	Cheerleading
Golf	Technology	Running
Cooking	Soccer	Weight Lifting
Band	Art	Hiking
Chess	Choir	Swimming
Science	Debate	Baseball
Karate	Volleyball	Shop

If you don't know of specific groups to join that match your top three interests, you might have to do a little leg work. Begin by asking a teacher or counselor for a list of all the clubs and organizations your school offers. Let's say you enjoy reading but your school doesn't have a book club, ask your English teacher if you can start one.

It might be the perfect opportunity for your leadership skills to shine.

The bottom line is that it's important to have friends whose company you enjoy and whose interests you share. Sometimes it might be appealing to form friendships with people because of the teams they are on, the clothes they wear or the crowd they run with. But such outward, **transient** qualities aren't always the best foundation to build a solid friendship. Make sure the friends you choose demonstrate the internal qualities you value. Are they empathetic? Are they kind? Are they willing to stand up for what they believe in? Listen to your instincts and gravitate toward the people whose values you respect and hopefully you'll forge relationships that will last a lifetime.

Transient *of short duration; not permanent*

Appreciate Differences

What about people who don't share your same passions and interests? Many people are fearful of those they don't understand, but lasting friendships can be **cultivated** between people who outwardly appear to have very little in common. It might just take a little effort in the beginning. Instead of avoiding or judging people who seem different from you, consider how you might be able to connect with and learn from their experiences. For example, maybe you have a classmate who comes from an unfamiliar background. While the two of you may practice different customs, you share commonalities, such as being the same age and having the same teacher. What else might you find in common

Cultivate *to nurture, foster, develop*

Friends can make your day,
especially when you are playing outside.

with this person as you get to know them? More importantly, what would you miss out on by not exploring this potential friendship? Consider how you could approach someone who is different than you and develop a friendship with them.

Friendships of this nature can be a bit more difficult to develop, but they often prove to be the richest, most enlightening relationships you'll have. It's one reason why so many people travel to foreign countries, so that they can experience other people and cultures. Seeing the world through someone else's perspective can teach you about them, the world around you, and perhaps most importantly, about yourself.

One of the easiest ways to forge a friendship with someone quite different than you is to ask a lot of questions. Most people are willing and eager to talk about themselves. And they often appreciate someone wanting to know more about them. Even if you don't become the best of friends, you'll learn new things and grow as a person. Challenging yourself to appreciate the differences of your classmates is a skill that will not only widen your social circle, but will help you in your adult life.

Thinking to Myself

There is a boy in my math class who sits off to the side by himself. He never talks to anyone. He keeps his head down, always looking at the ground. I think he just moved into the neighborhood a few weeks ago. I've noticed that when we have outdoor free time, he likes to shoot basketballs. He's pretty good at free throws. He must be a Lakers fan. He wears an LA jersey almost every day. I wonder if he likes math. He always seems to be the first to turn his work in, and then he just sits there and taps his pencil on his desktop. I feel like I should go introduce myself to him, but I have no idea what to say. I hate being shy.

1. How could this boy strike up a conversation with the student who is new to town? What questions could he ask?
2. How can this shy student benefit from reaching out to the new student?

Choose Friends Wisely

Middle school gives you the opportunity to choose many new friends and it's important to know how to choose wisely. You've read about gravitating toward people with common interests and personality qualities that you admire. It is also important to look for friends you respect and who respect you. Surrounding yourself with people who don't respect you can be draining. If you have friends who tease you, belittle you or fail to stand up for you, you may want to consider pulling away from the relationship. Standing up for yourself when you don't feel respected or treated properly is an important part of any healthy friendship.

At the same time, ensuring that you treat others the way you want to be treated is of utmost importance and is probably something you've heard about since you were very young. Known as the golden rule, it proves to be the best framework for being a great friend. When you're a good friend to others, they're more likely to treat you with respect and kindness.

While we're on the topic of choosing friends wisely, it is worth mentioning gangs. You've probably seen movies about people belonging to gangs, or may even know older kids who belong to one. Some teenagers choose to join gangs because they can provide a

Seeing Myself in Others

My name is Daniel. I've learned that to have a good friend you have to be a good friend. When I was in fifth grade, another student called me a nerd after seeing my report card with almost straight As. His comment made me feel self-conscious and a little embarrassed. In order to fit in, I began to get lower marks on purpose. I stopped turning in all of my homework and studying as much for tests. Another time, I saw a couple of kids bullying another student. They were pushing him, slapping him on the head, and calling him names. They urged me to join in, and I made the mistake of doing so. I've regretted it ever since.

My mom talked to me about being a leader and told me I didn't have to do what everyone else did. My step dad taught me to stand up for myself and what I believe in. They enrolled me in leadership classes, and I got to practice standing up to peer pressure. I learned how to be a leader by setting a good example, and my grades began improving again in sixth grade.

Whenever I see the kid I bullied, I make a point to be nice to him. I look for ways to help other students. If someone doesn't understand a problem in class, I offer to explain it to him or her. I've also helped the crossing guard at school and walked to school with younger kids to make sure they get there safely.

I try to find what I have in common with other people, and I like to encourage my friends to do the right thing. Being a good friend and leader is a lot better than just doing what everybody else is doing.

strong sense of belonging. However, gang members often engage in illegal and violent behaviors which can be dangerous or even **lethal**. And many former gang members agree that once you get involved with a gang it can be very difficult to separate from the group. Becoming a member of a gang can adversely affect your life

Lethal *ability to cause death; deadly*

forever, and therefore, it is critical that you choose your peer groups wisely. If you have questions or concerns about gangs, speak to your parents or school counselor.

WHAT HAVE YOU LEARNED?

Define *attribute*.

_____

_____

_____

Write a sentence about your own life using the word attribute.

_____

_____

_____

_____

Define *mutual*.

_____

_____

_____

Write a sentence about your own life using the word mutual.

_____

_____

_____

_____

Define *transient*.

_____

_____

_____

Write a sentence about your own life using the word transient.

_____

_____

_____

_____

Define *cultivate*.

_____

_____

_____

Write a sentence about your own life using the word cultivate.

_____

_____

_____

_____

Define *lethal*.

_____

_____

_____

Write a sentence about your own life using the word
lethal.

_____

_____

_____

_____

asking questions

REFLECT AND RESPOND

On a scale of 1—10, how important are friendships to
you? Why did you give this rating?

_____

_____

_____

_____

Describe one thing you struggle with in your friendships
and how you might improve in this area.

_____

_____

_____

_____

What does this make you think of?
Journal about your thoughts.

Developing Compassion

HOW DO YOU OPEN YOUR HEART?

s I stare out the school bus window, I worry about my grand-
ma. She's been so exhausted lately. I woke up last night to
the sound of her crying in the next room and found her sitting
with her head in her hands. She was surrounded by bills and papers,
upset about losing her health insurance. It was only two days ago that

51

I heard her tell one of my aunts that she wasn't making ends meet and that we might lose the house—the house in which my sisters and I have lived with her since our mother died six years ago. I'm afraid and I have no idea how to help her.

The bus stops and my friend John gets on, sliding into the seat next to me. "You seem quiet. Is everything okay?" he asks. "No," I think to myself, "things really aren't OK." Without warning, I begin to pour out my worries. John listens and asks me some questions. As I continue to tell him about everything that is happening, I begin to feel a little better. My troubles are still there, but it helps to have a friend care and listen.

Compassion is actively sympathizing with what others are experiencing—to recognize what they are feeling—and share in the experience. It allows us to open our hearts, to understand a difficult situation, and truly be there for someone in need. It is an attribute that makes the world a better place, starting right with your middle school. The following sections explore ways to become more compassionate.

This chapter is based on the work of David Richo, a successful author and psychotherapist, who suggests that applying the Five A's—attention, acceptance, appreciation, affection, and allowance—will help you become more compassionate, while allowing your relationships to grow and mature.

Attention

Attention is the gift you give to someone else when you're fully present. This type of attention is generally demonstrated through active listening and asking questions. Even something as simple as making or not making eye contact can indicate your level of interest.

Have you ever been talking to someone whose eyes flit around while you're talking, as though he or she is looking for someone passing by who might be more interesting than you? If you offer someone your attention, you stop what you are doing. It means you quit texting and put your phone down. You look them in the eye and focus on their words. You ask thoughtful ques-tions. Being able to fully listen to those who are important in your life demonstrates that you care about them. And it shows your ability to be compassionate. Learning to pay attention and devote this quality time to your family and friends strengthens these significant rela-tionships—because it's the quality, not just quantity, of the

Attention *applying the mind to something; concentration*

Working on your listening skills is important when you are struggling with your hardest subject

time spent with those important to you. The connection you feel in each of these relationships can only be improved when you take time to actively listen.

ACTIVITY

How attentive do you think you are in the following situations? Rate your ability to be a good listener using a scale of one to ten (one being the lowest and ten being the highest).

_____ 1. When you are in class

_____ 2. When you are at family meals

_____ 3. When you are with friends at lunch

_____ 4. When you are sad

_____ 5. When you are excited

_____ 6. When you are bored

_____ 7. When you are confused

_____ 8. When you are tired

_____ 9. When you are angry

_____10. When you feel slighted

Stopping to think about your ability to listen in these situations can help you determine ways to improve your attention. Everyone occasionally gets wrapped up in their own worlds at times, but if you repeatedly tune others out, it negatively affects your ability to be compassionate. How can you be more attentive and truly listening to others when you interact?

_____

_____

_____

Thinking to Myself

My friend left class crying today. Whispers broke out across the room when she got up to leave. It took me a while to find her during our lunch period. I finally spotted her sitting by herself under a tree behind the building. I asked her what was wrong. She told me her dog was being put to sleep after school. All the warning signs her family had been noticing over the past few months now had a name: cancer. I felt horrible for her. She was only three when her parents brought the puppy home. She and the dog had practically been raised together. I can only imagine how much she'll miss him. I put my arms around her while she cried.

1. How do you think this girl would have reacted had her friend taken out a cell phone and sent a text message during their conversation?

2. How do you feel when you are around someone who is upset? Does it make you uncomfortable? What is the value of pursuing a friend who is upset and asking them if they want to talk?

Acceptance

Another way to develop compassion is through acceptance. When you embrace people for who they are, without making assumptions based on outward appearances, you are accepting them. As you share and make discoveries about your differences with others, positive changes can emerge in your school and your community.

However, acceptance involves more than simply being nice to someone you wouldn't normally associate with at school. It involves recognizing both the positive and the negative characteristics in others, and then making the choice to take them as they are without trying to change them. People you love and care about might disappoint you at times, just

Acceptance *the act of receiving something or someone graciously*

as you might occasionally disappoint them. But no one is perfect, and as a result, there are times when accepting others as they are, in spite of their shortcomings, is important to be able to do.

Imagine you have a teacher who is wonderfully entertaining, funny and full of life—someone who teaches you so much about your world. But what if they are unorganized and fail to return your work to you in a timely manner? Do you ask to be removed from the class and deny yourself the experience of learning from this fabulous teacher? Or is it worth accepting this person? Being able to embrace those we care about, in spite of their shortcomings, can help develop our sense of compassion while opening up new worlds.

Appreciation

While acceptance might involve overlooking the negative in someone, appreciation emphasizes acknowledging the positive. You express compassion when you are able to acknowledge others. And you may find that the ability to be appreciative, to find gratitude, is one of the greatest gifts you can give to yourself.

Acknowledge the strengths of your friends. You can be part of a wonderful, diverse team.

Sometimes the simplest thank you can mean the most. How do you show your appreciation for those who do things for you? Do you tell your parents thank you for preparing your favorite meal? Do you acknowledge your friend's wonderful listening skills after she's helped you out with a relationship problem? Have you ever sent a coach a thank you card for pushing you to be your best? For the next week, try to thank or acknowledge three people each day who extend themselves for you. This activity is a great way to reflect on what's being given to you, while helping you develop compassion for those who positively influence your world.

Appreciation *to recognize the value of something or someone*

It can be hard at times to appreciate others when there is tension between you. Perhaps you have a younger brother who wants to spend more time together. When your patience runs low, you may get angry and ignore or avoid him. Yet what might it look like if you appreciate the fact that he wants to spend time with you? How might he respond if you tell him you are grateful he wants to be with you, but that you have other things you must do first? What if you commit to giving him some attention a little later if he agrees to give you the time and space you need now? Perhaps honoring his desires and acknowledging his wishes will help him be patient and give you the time you need as well.

Affection

Thinking to Myself

I'm terrible about telling people I love them. I get annoyed when my parents come to check on me after I get in bed or when my grandparents, who don't even live in town, try to hug or kiss me when they come visit. It has nothing to do with being "at that age" or anything, because I've always been this way. I hope they know I value my relationships even though I don't always show it. It's just not my way. But sometimes I wonder if I'm hurting them.

1.) How could this student express feelings towards his family in ways that would be comfortable for him?

2.) How do you show the important people in your life that you value them?

Affection can be described as fondness or tender feelings you have for others. Hopefully, you have affection for many people in your life. Animals might also be the recipients of your affection. Affection can be demonstrated in many ways—verbally, physically, and emotionally. A smile of encouragement to a younger brother successfully shooting his first basket demonstrates affection. A hug for a friend who's just learned of their grandmother's death shows you care. Or telling your father you missed him when he returns from a business trip is a way to express your feelings.

Affection *to show tenderness, warmth, love, devotion or kindness*

Have you ever had a puppy jump in your lap and lick you with kisses? An animal's expression of affection is a wonderful thing. And scientific research shows that people who receive the love of animals tend to live longer lives. Everyone benefits from demonstrating and receiving affection, yet it can be difficult to know how to express it, especially during your teenage years.

How you show affection changes with time. When you were younger, you were most likely very affectionate with

your parents. Holding their hands, climbing in their laps, and cuddling with them on the couch were probably regular routines for you. As a teenager, however, you may begin to want more space from them, especially when other people are around. Although it can be hard to balance your family's need of reassurance as you pull away with a desire for greater personal space, it's something you'll learn how to manage with time.

Remember there are ways to show you care that might be more comfortable for you now. Saying thank you goes a long way. It shows you both acknowledge and appreciate what a loved one has done for you. What about making the effort to ask your mom how her day was? What about sneaking a note into your sister's lunch, letting her know you're thinking of her? These are just a few simple ways to demonstrate your affection. Developing the awareness and ability to express these emotions will help you become a more mature, compassionate person.

Allowance

In order to have a mature, compassionate relationship with another person, you must allow him or her room to grow outside of your relationship—just as he or she must give you room to grow. When you're in middle school, perhaps having a tougher time making friends than you've ever had before, it can be tempting to desire the security that having a single best friend can bring. A best friend can be more appealing than a group of friends

Seeing Myself in Others

My name is Auriel. I love reading and writing poetry. Poetry is a way for me to express myself because I'm a shy person, and I tend to write more when I'm stressed out and feeling down. My poems are usually about whatever I'm going through at the time I put them down on paper, and they help me get in touch with my feelings. When I read poems by others, I'm able to put myself in their shoes and feel more empathy for them.

I was overweight in elementary school and sometimes kids made fun of me. I have a much better body image today, but many of the poems I wrote back then were about how I felt when I was teased. I've always tried to encourage others to be considerate and appreciate all of the people who help build them up. One of my favorite poems I've written is called, "Looking at My Reflection." It's about how I see myself and how I perceive that other people see me. I don't share my poems with many people besides my best friend, Korey. I trust her, and we've known each other since the fourth grade. Sometimes we write poems together.

My plan is to major in early childhood education at Roosevelt University in Chicago and become an elementary school teacher. While I was in high school, I took an early childhood education class at a local community college. It helped confirm my interest in teaching, and someday I'd like to open my own day care facility and share my love of poetry with children and young people. I hope it will enrich their lives as much as it has mine and help them develop a strong sense of compassion for what others are experiencing.

because you feel more valued as a companion, and you have more control over the levels of drama and competition when there are just two of you involved. But friendships can be stifling when people don't allow one another to pursue other relationships and interests. Encourage your friends to learn more about themselves as you make discoveries about who you are inside. In the long run, such encouragement usually strengthens the bonds or relationships.

Allowance *partly excusing an offense, mistake or shortcoming*

The Five A's and Compassion

Hopefully looking at compassion, through the lens of these Five A's, helps you understand specific ways in which you can become more compassionate and enrich your relationships. Focusing on being more attentive, appreciative, accepting and allowing, while learning to express your affection for those you love in ways that make you comfortable, will add to the richness of your life. By making the effort to demonstrate these qualities in your day-to-day life, you'll be certain to see others reciprocate these behaviors to you.

Define *attention*.

_____

_____

_____

Write a sentence about your own life using the word attention.

_____

_____

_____

_____

Define *acceptance*.

_____

_____

_____

Write a sentence about your own life using the word acceptance.

_____

_____

_____

_____

Define *appreciation*.

_____

_____

_____

Write a sentence about your own life using the word appreciation.

_____

_____

_____

_____

Define *affection*.

_____

_____

_____

Write a sentence about your own life using the word affection.

_____

_____

_____

_____

Define *allowance*.

_____

_____

_____

Write a sentence about your own life using the word allowance.

_____

_____

_____

_____

asking questions

Which of the five A's is the easiest for you to demonstrate? Why?

_____

_____

_____

_____

_____

Which of the Five A's is most difficult for you to practice? Why? How can you improve it?

_____

_____

_____

_____

_____

What specifically can you do to become more compassionate at home? What can you do to become more compassionate at school?

_____

_____

_____

_____

_____

In what areas do you wish others were able to show you greater compassion?

_____

_____

_____

_____

_____

Handling Your Relationships

HOW DO YOU CONNECT WITH OTHERS?

ook what Amy is wearing." Natasha says. I hear her comment over the dull hum of the cafeteria as I approach the popular girls' table. Plates clatter. Students giggle. My heart skips a beat. A remark delivered in that tone is never meant as a compliment. I slow my pace as I frantically try to figure out what's wrong with my

67

outfit. With each step, I feel more eyes turning to watch me. A knot of panic works its way into my stomach. I reach to put my tray down on the table. "Natasha, aren't we saving that chair for Ashley?" Maria asks abruptly as I approach the only empty seat. "Yeah," Natasha responds, looking up at me with a cold stare, "We are. Sorry Amy," she throws in flippantly. My feet feel like lead as tears begin to well up in my eyes. I smile anyway, trying to hide my hurt and confusion. I turn around and walk in the opposite direction, acting as though Maria and Natasha's table is just one of many I want to join. I can't help but wonder what's wrong with what I'm wearing. "Tell me the rules," I want to scream. But I know they just make them up as they go along. And who makes them the fashion police? I know I shouldn't take it personally, but I want to be part of their group. I try to keep my head high, but I can still hear them laughing.

Peers

You meet a lot of new people in middle school, even if you enter with a group of friends from elementary school. Some of these people are fun, some cruel, some annoying, and hopefully, some inspiring. You might not be able to get a correct reading on everyone right away, but in time you'll begin to see who appeals to you and why they might make a good friend. Choosing friends that you respect and respect you will be part of the middle school challenge. You just might meet some of the very best friends of your life. But chances are you won't reach the end of middle school without a few emotional bumps and bruises along the way.

You'll notice that some of the students you'll meet over the next few years will change very little as they move through middle school. Unfortunately, some of the girls

who acted **maliciously** toward Amy in the story at the beginning of the chapter may continue to treat others in a similar fashion when they become adults. On the other hand, some of the other girls who were mean to Amy might have simply been going through a phase, flirting with the power that comes with being popular. The point is, you'll be surrounded by people you like and people you don't like. Learning how to interact and get along with these different groups will be your challenge.

Malicious *vicious, spiteful, harmful, or mischievous in motivation*

There will be times you'll wish you could change the behavior of others. And while this might not be possible, you can adjust your attitude to **accommodate** certain difficult situations. Amy couldn't keep Natasha from making snide remarks about her outfit; however, she could choose how to respond. Standing up for herself, she might have said, "Well I like what I'm wearing," or "I'm sorry there isn't a seat available here. I'll join Mary and Keisha today." Generally, these difficult students are looking for your reaction. If they see they've knocked you down, they feel victorious in their behavior. But if you

Accommodate *to adapt or make fit; to do a favor*

simply move on, and keep your attitude positive and focused, you'll hold onto your power in these trying situations. Doing this is not easy. Learning to handle negative things people say and do to you is a life-long lesson. But with each instance you have the opportunity to step forward, learn more about who you are and make **conscious** choices about who you want to be.

Conscious *to be aware of, awake; alert*

Are you familiar with the queen bee and schoolyard bully stereotypes? Do you know how to spot these types? Do you know how to avoid them? Bullies and queen bees often demonstrate toxic behavior, frequently using peer pressure to manipulate others into participating in hurtful, dangerous activities that demean people. They often have contagious personalities with an aggressive streak.

Here are some examples of toxic behavior:

1. The person becomes threatened if you challenge their way of thinking.
2. The person pressures you into doing things that they want.
3. The person threatens to withhold their acceptance of you unless you do things or think of things in their way.
4. The person feels a need to compete with you, trying to appear superior.
5. The person demands you prove yourself over and over again.
6. The person constantly volleys for the center of attention.

When you encounter bullies remind yourself that they are often belittling you in attempts to make themselves

Cultivate strong friendships with positive supportive people.

feel tougher. Even though they present an intimidating front, bullies are usually insecure. It can help to remember that these challenging people are dealing with the same changes as you are, and that they might be experiencing troubles outside of school. Having compassion for such students, while making sure to stand up for yourself, can be a fine line to walk. If you ever feel a situation with a bully is escalating out of control, or if you are physically threatened in any manner, be certain to immediately inform a teacher or another adult.

Queen bees share many characteristics with bullies. Girls who become queen bees seek out admiration and support in order to feel powerful. They, too, are often trying to mask feelings of insecurity, and deal with this by gaining popularity based on external characteristics such as looks, clothing, and attitude. However, the life of a queen bee can be very difficult as she strives to keep up her image. Once again, trying to have compassion for what might be motivating someone to operate in this way may help you deal with their challenging behavior. But the same rule applies. If you notice situations becoming over-ly cruel, violent or dangerous, seek out the help of a counselor, teacher or adult.

Thinking to Myself

Three weeks ago, someone I thought was my friend started sending me text messages saying I am a horrible person. Then I started hearing things I had said in confidence whispered among my classmates. Several of my personal secrets I had shared were being posted online. Then people started saying things about me that weren't true. Now all I can think about are these rumors. I know my parents would support me if I told them about what was going on, but I'm afraid of getting people in trouble at school. I can only imagine what the other kids would say then.

1. How do you see this bullying behavior escalating?
2. If you were this student, how would you handle the above situation?

One of the difficult things about bullying is that it may not stop when the bell rings at the end of the day. Now that you're in middle school, your parents may have started to loosen some of the restrictions placed on your level of Internet use. Other kids' parents have probably started to loosen up as well, and you may have noticed more and more cell phones popping up at school. As you and your peers gain increased access to technology, cyber-bullying can quickly become a big problem. Cyber-bullying can be defined as threatening, harassing, or humiliating another through e-mail, text messaging, instant messaging, blogging, webpage postings, etc. These destructive actions can be emotionally devastating.

If you are the recipient of cyber-bullying, don't immediately return the messages or respond online to the postings. Messages returned in anger may only escalate the problem. Rather than immediately return insults, see if you can initiate a face to face discussion with the perpetrator if you know who it is. If the bullying continues or is ever threatening, let your parents know immediately. In addition, keep a record of evidence. If you don't know who the cyber-bully is, inform your parents or a trusted adult. Depending on the severity, you may want to notify your school, the Internet Service Provider, and the police.

Authorities in cyber-bullying prevention suggest you should also take the following actions.

1. Keep your personal information private so no one can impersonate you or break into your online accounts.

2. Conduct an online search for your name. You'll be able to find out if anyone is posing as you on the Internet, and then you can alert the website and have the profile taken down.

3. Ask your friends why they want you to post something or set up a website. They could be using you in order to hurt someone else.

4. Remember the golden rule: don't do anything to someone online that you wouldn't want done to you.

Source: www.stopcyberbullying.org

Teams

Getting along with others goes well beyond dealing with bullies and queen bees. Sometimes it involves working with a group on a project or participating on a team. For the rest of your life you'll be required to work well with others in some type of capacity. And this remains a challenge for many adults. It is believed that the number one reason adults are fired from jobs is because they fail to get along with others. So middle school is the perfect arena to develop skills for working well with others.

What makes a team successful? Is it strong leadership? Does it involve having members who know how to follow direction effectively? Does it require teammates being aware of their strengths and weaknesses and knowing how to best handle these? What about mutual support and encouragement? Does it involve reaching out to those who are reluctant to participate? All of these factors contribute to a team's success.

In middle school you may find that teachers emphasize collaborative learning where you are required to complete projects in groups. As you encounter these situations ask yourself how you can be the best team player possible. If you are shy and not the best candidate for presenting your findings in front of the class, can you offer to put the information in writing for the team? Or perhaps you can agree to be the communications "expert" for the group, making sure everyone knows when and where each meeting will be held. Always look for an area where you can best contribute.

Sometimes the best teammates are the ones who know how to encourage others. Creating positive energy amongst the group is extremely important. Take it upon yourself to ensure your teammates feel good about their contributions. If you have a member who remains on the perimeter, failing to participate, see if you can pull him or her into the group. Sometimes this can be easily done by simply

Bring your best efforts to your team to produce the best outcomes possible.

asking, "What would you like to work on?" Or you might suggest they pair up with another to work on a specific task. Explore what works and what doesn't, knowing this might change from group to group.

Family

$\mathcal{T}$hinking to $\mathcal{M}$yself

My dad is always away on business. Sometimes he's gone for five or six days a week. I used to wish he was around more spending time with me, getting to know some of my friends and taking me places, but lately I've started to not like it when he comes home. My parents fight because he's never around to help my mom with the house and us kids. He disrupts our routine when he returns from a trip in the middle of the week. I know I should be grateful for the good money he earns by leaving all the time, but I often feel angry at him. I'm ashamed of myself for feeling this way, and I'm confused.

1. Why do you think this student feels conflicted about the relationship with his father?

2. If this were you, what specific steps might you take to improve this relationship?

Your most challenging relationships may be at home rather than at school. Some of the hardest people to get along with can be your family members. Perhaps you take your anger out on them when you've had a bad day because you know they'll stick with you for better or worse. Or maybe your older siblings tease you as you begin puberty. Younger siblings may demand time and attention you're unwilling to give because you now have other things you want to do.

However, one of the most challenging aspects of middle school can be the changing relationship you'll have with your parents. At this point in your life you will be acquiring more independence while at the same time more will be expected of you in middle school. These changes can cause shifts in your relationships at home.

Navigating these shifts depends on the type of relationship you currently have with your mom and/or dad. If you come from a home with very few rules and demands, you made need to structure your time and impose rules on yourself, otherwise meeting the increased demands of middle school will be difficult. If your parents are very strict, you might have to make extra efforts to communicate with them and prove your ability to manage new areas of your life, thereby winning their trust and confidence.

If you have a parent that is not around much, it helps to communicate and keep them informed as much as possible. Many parents today are juggling work, taking care of children, paying the bills, caring for their own aging parents, and personal health issues. While in an ideal world they'd give you 100% of their time and attention, in reality it is not possible. As your middle school demands gear up, you can help create a win-win situation with your parents by communicating as much as you can about your education, social, physical and emotional needs.

Finally, if you have parents who hover and are over-involved in your life, you'll have to slowly move out from under their wings so that you can become your own person. This process can be difficult for both you and your parents. It's hard for mothers and fathers to let go after they've put their children front and center of their own lives. It can be equally hard to assume new responsibil-

ities for yourself as a teen after your parents have picked up the pieces of your life and have fought your battles for you for years. Yet if you strive to assume responsibility for yourself and help your parents develop confidence in you, the shift can gradually take place.

Some students are faced with the extra challenge of having parents who are ill—either physically or emotionally. If this is your case, you'll need to balance being supportive of your parent(s), while maintaining the space in your life to do well in school and the other areas that will affect your future. This fine line can be hard to walk,

Seeing Myself in Others

My name is Maggie. I just completed fifth grade, and next year will be my first year of middle school. I enjoy working with all kinds of people, and I always try to put my best into relationships. When I'm with other kids, I go out of my way to be friendly because I appreciate when people do that for me. There's a girl in my class who sometimes treats me disrespectfully, but I don't retaliate because I know it won't help. When I'm with adults, I try to act in a way that makes them remember me as someone who was nice to work with rather than as someone who was a pain in the neck.

I recently returned from spending a week at the Junior National Young Leaders Conference in Washington, D.C. My homeroom teacher nominated me and one other student from my class to attend this event based on our academic and leadership potential. It was scary when I first got there because I didn't know anyone and most of the other kids did. They were so preoccupied with the friends they already had that I felt like an outsider. But that night I got to know my roommates, and I kept introducing myself to new people. By the third day, I felt comfortable at the conference.

When I think about starting middle school next year, I get a little nervous. The building is big because it's a middle school and high school combined. I've always liked to have a close relationship with just one teacher, and I wonder if I'll like having several teachers. But since I like working with people, I'm sure things will be all right. I'll look at starting middle school pretty much like I do everything else: as one big adventure.

and any additional support you can garner from counselors and teachers will help.

Every family has its own set of challenges. Unfortunately there may be times your needs won't be met. You may have only one parent, or perhaps you live with people other than your parents. The key is to find people in your life to support and honor you. It may be a teacher, an older sibling or an aunt or uncle. Learning to work with your situation at home is a lifelong skill you can begin to develop in middle school. And while it may be challenging at times, these years will create an opportunity to become even closer with those you love.

Authority Figures Outside the Home

As you grow and mature, the opportunity to develop relationships with adults outside of your family increases. Your core teachers continue to play a huge role in your development. Coaches, club advisors, extracurricular teachers and school administrators may also influence you during these years. It is critical to learn how to work well with these figures and cultivate supportive relationships with them. It won't be long before you're looking for letters of reference as you apply for jobs, high schools and colleges. Some of the adults you encounter now may be your greatest allies in the future.

Challenge yourself to reach out to these significant adults. Go talk to a teacher if you struggle in his class. He will appreciate the effort you make in asking for assistance, and by doing this, you show initiative.

When working with adults, remember to demonstrate respect. You can do this by showing up on time for appoint-

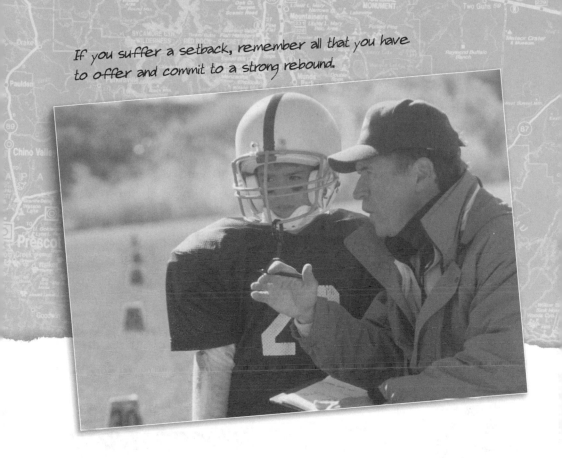

If you suffer a setback, remember all that you have to offer and commit to a strong rebound.

ments, staying committed to your agreements, being fully attentive and showing compassion. Exhibiting respectful behavior not only impresses adults you encounter, it helps ensure that you'll be treated in return with the greatest respect possible.

While things might be challenging, try to keep an open mind. Years from now you may look back and realize that what your cross country coach taught you did not only **pertain** to running or racing. Maybe it had more to do with keeping negative thoughts from limiting your success. By keeping an open mind, you can maximize your learning from the significant adults in your life.

Pertain *to relate; to be connected as a part*

School counselors are another important resource you can turn to for help. You may not be very familiar with your counselors but don't let this lack of acquaintance **deter** you from seeking help. In some cases, not knowing your counselor personally can be beneficial, especially if you need someone to talk to in confidence about problems you're having with your peers or teachers. Counselors are also a useful resource you can consult if you're unsatisfied with your schedule, need help planning for high school or finding extracurricular activities you'd like to pursue. These people are professionally trained to help students like you, and if they can't give you the help you require, they can direct you to someone who can.

Deter *to turn aside, discourage or prevent from acting*

vocabulary

WHAT HAVE YOU LEARNED?

Define *malicious*.

_____

_____

_____

Write a sentence about your own life using the word malicious.

_____

_____

_____

Define *accommodate*.

_____

_____

_____

Write a sentence about your own life using the word
accommodate.

_____

_____

_____

_____

Define *conscious*.

_____

_____

_____

Write a sentence about your own life using the word
conscious.

_____

_____

_____

_____

Define *pertain*.

_____

_____

_____

Write a sentence about your own life using the word pertain.

_____

_____

_____

_____

Define *deter*.

_____

_____

_____

Write a sentence about your own life using the word deter.

_____

_____

_____

_____

asking questions

REFLECT AND RESPOND

When and where have you witnessed toxic behavior? Was it your own or someone else's?

_____

_____

_____

_____

What would you do if a bully approached you, said something negative, and/or physically hurt you?

_____

_____

_____

_____

_____

If you've bullied someone, what could you do to rectify the situation?

_____

_____

_____

_____

_____

What does this make you think of?
Journal about your thoughts.

Healthy Boundaries

HOW DO YOU SET APPROPRIATE LIMITS?

y hands begin to sweat. I follow the other boys out of the locker room after the first day of basketball practice. We step outside and I lean against the brick wall behind the gym. I'm happy to finally become part of this group of guys. They've all played together for years and know each other well. It's been hard being the newcomer. Justin, by far the tallest and clearly the group leader, grins after scanning the area for onlookers. He pulls out a pack of cigarettes from his pocket. My heart beats faster as he passes it around. Each boy takes one. Justin looks my way and says, "Want one, Kevin?" I've never been faced with this kind of decision. I've always believed I'd never smoke. I saw my grandfather struggle for years trying to quit. He now has Emphysema. Besides, I'm an athlete and I want to take care of my body. I ignore the sick feeling in my stomach. I accept a cigarette, put it in my mouth, and allow Justin to light it.

Defining Boundaries

What does the term boundary suggest to you? Webster's Dictionary defines it as something that marks a limit or border. You've all been subject to boundaries most of your life. You may have been told, "No television until your homework is complete," or "You must have my permission before using the Internet." These boundaries determine rules or guidelines for expected behavior.

You also may have experienced internal boundaries that reflect your thoughts and feelings. Perhaps a friend has gossiped about you, telling a secret of yours behind your back. If you trusted this friend and this trust has been broken, you might decide to no longer share personal information with this person. In doing so you establish an internal boundary that is not to be crossed or violated.

Your boundaries reflect what you value, think and feel. They also help determine the actions you take. So great care must be given to both the internal and external boundaries you create. This process will be one of the greatest challenges and opportunities you'll face in middle school. Up to this point, your parents and teachers set the majority of boundaries that shape your life. Now is the time for you to start setting some of your own.

This chapter opens with the story of Kevin, a student eager to bond with a new group of friends. He is tested by an invitation to cross a personal boundary—his belief that he'd never smoke. Should he hold onto his values of physical health and fitness, or loosen his boundary to fit in with new friends?

Thinking to Myself

My friend knows the combination to my locker. She often goes through my things when I'm not there and fails to put them back where they belong. She took my lip gloss one day. Another time she borrowed a textbook I needed for class and looked at my homework without asking. Sometimes she even takes food out of my lunch bag. Today I had the combination to my locker changed without telling her. I'm afraid of what she's going to say, but she never listens to me when I ask her to stop getting into my things. I really want my privacy back.

1. Do you believe this student should change her locker combination? Why or why not?

2. If this were you, how would you approach the friend who's been going through your belongings?

How to Set Boundaries

M any boundaries are set to **safeguard** you from phys-ical or emotional harm. The boundary of wearing a helmet when you skateboard can protect you from getting a concussion, where as a boundary to keep your distance from a classmate who **manipulates** you and copies off your work will help protect your integrity. The challenge then becomes setting appropriate boundaries and knowing when and how to tighten or loosen these limits.

Safeguard *to protect and secure*

Manipulate *to manage or control the action of something*

The following diagram, based on the work of Pia Mcllody, illustrates a variety of bound-aries. As you can see, there can be positive and negative boundaries.

RIGID boundaries   NO boundaries   HEALTHY boundaries

Rigid Boundaries

I t's both **counterproductive** and unhealthy to have boundaries that function as unmoving, impassable stone walls. Some people build such walls to protect themselves from getting hurt, but this isolation might keep you from experiencing

Counterproductive *hinder the attainment of an intended goal*

life to the fullest. Be conscious of your needs and feelings, and of course your personal health and safety, but allow yourself the opportunity to step out of your comfort zone when it is appropriate. Stretching yourself can be a tremendous way to build self-respect and help you learn to set healthy boundaries that both protect you and allow you to grow.

Some examples of rigid boundaries include:

- Sam recently became a vegetarian and no longer eats meat or chicken. His friend invites him over for dinner. He refuses the invitation because he worries they may serve him meat. How can Sam honor the commitment he's made to himself while keeping his boundaries flexible?

This friend fully accepts her friend who is a snake-lover!

- Mary is friendly to her classmates but refuses to develop alliances with anyone who doesn't practice her religion. How do you think Mary's life might be limited by this strict boundary?

- Joe's closest friend from elementary school has moved into a new peer group. His friend made plans for the weekend with this group, excluding Joe. What made things worse is that he lied to Joe about what he was doing. Joe swears that he'll never be close to this boy again. Do you believe Joe's boundary is appropriate? Why or why not?

Loose Boundaries

While it is important at times to keep your boundaries flexible so that you have the opportunity to grow and evolve, overly loose or no boundaries can cause trouble. Have you ever had friends that take advantage of you over and over again? Perhaps they copy your homework, cheat off your test, and beg you to help them with their work when you know they aren't trying themselves. By not establishing a limit on how much you'll help these friends, you can begin to feel "walked on." Resentment builds and can ultimately cause you to break off these friendships. In this instance, a firm boundary must be placed on what you are willing to do and what you are not willing to do for these people. Knowing where and how to set these limits is critical for your personal development.

Loose boundaries can take many different forms. Here are some examples:

- Meisha talks to everyone about her thoughts and feelings. And she constantly shares her most personal stories with people she just meets. She gets frustrated when other kids talk about the problems she's shared with them. What do you think Meisha should do?

- Everywhere Luke goes, he has his phone in his hand. He sends over two hundred text messages a day. His grades are dropping because it's hard for him to concentrate on his studies while being interrupted by a barrage of text messages. His parents have threatened to take away his phone. What boundaries could Luke set for himself?

- Kara loves fashion. She works long hours babysitting so that she can buy the clothes and jewelry she likes. Her older sister often sneaks into her room and borrows her things. Last week she broke Kara's favorite earrings. Kara is frustrated and tired of hiding her belongings from her sister. What should Kara do?

Ignoring Your Boundaries

Have you ever ignored your personal boundaries, acting in a way that contradicts your beliefs and standards you've set for yourself? What happens when you say yes to something while your insides are screaming no? Your breathing might get faster or your heart may start to pound. Perhaps you don't experience a physical reaction in such instances, but your **intuition** tells you something isn't right. You might simply hear a small voice inside questioning how you've reacted or responded to a situation. These are all signals that are important to heed.

Intuition *to have instinctive knowledge or feeling*

Your thoughts, feelings and values are measures you use to establish healthy boundaries. So if things aren't

Seeing Myself in Others

My name is Brande. During my teen years, I was faced with a choice that had serious consequences. One of my best friends lived on a local military base, and sometimes we would visit the base store to buy a snack or hang out for a while. One day, my friend told me she had found a free way to get music: by stealing CDs from the base store.

Even as I contemplated the possible trouble we could get in, I followed my friend into the store the next afternoon. I watched her put two CDs in her purse. Almost instantly, a police officer came rushing towards us, grabbed her arm, and told us both to come to the store office. The officer called her parents, and my friend ended up having to go to court. Luckily, the store manager didn't press charges against me because I hadn't taken anything.

From this experience, I learned to be aware of how other people influence me and how quickly circumstances can spiral out of control. My friend's decision to steal not only jeopardized her reputation —it jeopardized mine, too. I've also learned to trust my instincts. When I felt uncomfortable going into the store that day, or even the day before when my friend first told me she was stealing CDs, I could have protested. I could have told her I wouldn't shoplift and asked her if we could come up with a better way to get free music.

Healthy boundaries put you in charge of your own life rather than letting someone or something else control it. If I had learned earlier to maintain a strong sense of who I was, what I valued, and what I felt comfortable with, I would have been able to avoid a potentially dangerous situation.

feeling right, check in with yourself by asking "Are my boundaries too rigid or am I being pushed to do or give something that doesn't feel appropriate to me?" Being able to **differentiate** in these instances will help you establish

Differentiate *make a distinction between*

effective limits for yourself. These limits, in turn, will help you respond appropriately and get what you need from others, while also helping others know how to treat and respond to you.

Most students experience some form of peer pressure in middle school. You may feel pressure from friends to dress a certain way, to treat others in a manner you might not agree with, to experiment with drugs or alcohol, or simply to do things that don't feel right to you. Imagine it is Halloween night and your new friends are begging you to watch a horror movie, but you know that if you do . . . you will have nightmares

for weeks. You don't want to appear immature to your friends, but you don't want to be sleepless for weeks. What do you do?

Or, what if you're working on a group project and one of your teammates wants to plagiarize a report from the internet? Chances are you won't be the only one feeling persuaded by such peer pressure. If you have the courage to stand up and hold true to what is best for you, others will often follow your lead and respect you. And if not, you'll at least respect yourself.

Now is the perfect time in your life to start listening to your own instincts so that you can choose your actions and reactions to the situations you encounter. Practicing this process will ultimately help you differentiate between positive and negative choices, between responsible and irresponsible risks, and between healthy and unhealthy relationships.

Thinking to Myself

My parents just got divorced and my dad moved into an apartment nearby. I knew it would be hard adjusting to these changes but didn't foresee half the problems. Both of my parents now try to be way too involved in my life. They compete for my attention. Because they don't have each other anymore, they want to spend all their time with me. I haven't been able to see my friends as much since they split up and all I want is a little space. I need time to think about things other than my parent's divorce.

1. What boundaries are being violated here?
2. What do you think this student can do to help his parents become aware of how he's feeling?

vocabulary

Define *safeguard*.

_____

_____

_____

Write a sentence about your own life using the word
safeguard.

_____

_____

_____

_____

Define *manipulate*.

_____

_____

_____

Write a sentence about your own life using the word
manipulate.

_____

_____

_____

_____

Define *counterproductive.*

_____

_____

_____

Write a sentence about your own life using the word
counterproductive.

_____

_____

_____

_____

Define *intuition.*

_____

_____

_____

Write a sentence about your own life using the word
intuition.

_____

_____

_____

_____

Define *differentiate.*

_____

_____

_____

Write a sentence about your own life using the word differentiate.

_____

_____

_____

_____

asking questions

Consider this alternate ending to Kevin's story:

> I ignore the sick feeling in my stomach as I try to make a joke. "I smoked a few times last year and it stunted my growth." There's a pause—or do I only imagine it? Then they laugh, and I laugh with them. "That's cool, Kevin," Justin says, and I feel wonderful.

Write your own alternate ending to Kevin's story. How else could he have handled the situation?

_____

_____

_____

_____

_____

_____

_____

Write about a time you didn't maintain healthy boundaries. What was the outcome?

_____

_____

_____

_____

_____

_____

Write about a time you asserted yourself to maintain
your boundaries. What did you say? What happened?

_____

_____

_____

_____

_____

What does this make you think of?
Journal about your thoughts.

PART III

Personal Life

Nurturing Your Brain and Body

HOW CAN YOU BE YOUR BEST?

A s my homeroom teacher moves down the attendance list, I sigh. I think about how somewhere, in another homeroom class, my brother's name is being called. I know he doesn't answer. He didn't go to school again today, faking sick, because he wants to do drugs while my parents are at work. I hate the smell of the air freshener he sprays to mask the scent of the marijuana. I wish one of my parents would arrive home before me just once. I'm afraid to tell on him. From my desk, I look around at my friends and class-mates and feel ashamed of myself and of my family. I know my brother's hurting himself physically, as well as academically, but I don't know what to do.

The Brain

*I*f you ever need a new kidney or liver, it's possible to have a transplant. No similar procedure exists for a brain. The brain you have now is the one you'll have forever, which is why it's so important to take good care of it. You have the power to make your brain the best it can be.

The story above is disturbing because it describes a student consciously hurting his brain. One of the easiest ways you can keep your brain healthy is by avoiding drugs and alcohol. You've probably been told for years to wear a helmet when you ride a bicycle or skateboard. Injuries resulting from hard falls can also adversely affect the brain, hindering you the rest of your life. It is impor-tant for you to do all you can to protect your brain.

Think of the ways you use a computer. Computers allow you to store data and files so that you can easily find them later. Through the Internet, you have access to more information than you could ever possibly want, need, use, or remember. Computers also allow you to communicate with people all over the world. And if you want to express your creativity, computer programs can help you generate aesthetic results.

Now consider some of the ways that you use your brain. The human brain is a wonderfully complex organ that can perform all of the above functions and more. It, too, specializes in the access and retrieval of information, helping you to recall names, faces, dates, formulas, and memories. Your brain also helps you create new ideas and express your feelings and experiences in ways all your own. It helps you solve complex problems, read people's emotions and organize your muscles so that you can bike, swim and run.

At the same time, your brain is the director of a large communication network. Every time you blink, walk, sweat, or digest the pizza you ate for lunch, it's because your brain has instructed your muscles, organs, glands, and other body parts to do so. For instance, even though

Mack uses a vision board to help her imagine and then define a class project about Whoopi Goldberg.

a strong heart is essential to your survival, a healthy heart gets you nowhere if you do not have an even higher-functioning brain to regulate it.

Likewise, brain activity monitors and directs your breathing rate, muscle coordination, body temperature, sleep, consciousness, reflexes, and secretion of hormones. It processes your emotions, senses, and perception of pain while helping you engage in higher forms of thinking and creative pursuits. Everything you do involves your brain. So you can see why it is of utmost importance to take the best care of it possible.

How the Brain Works

You may have learned that the cell is the basis of every life form on Earth. You have muscle cells, blood cells, skin cells, along with others. The brain, which is part of your nervous system, is composed of tiny nerve cells called **neurons,** whose main purpose is to transmit messages to the rest of the cells in your body.

While the next several paragraphs are a bit complicated, see if you can follow how these brain cells, or neurons, act as communicators from the brain to the body.

Neuron *a cell that is the basic unit of the nervous system and which conducts nerve impulses*

Dendrites: *branches from the bodies of neurons that receive and transmit nerve impulses*

Each neuron contains a nucleus which is the control center of the cell. In addition, each neuron has a mass of **dendrites** that branches out from the cell body. The dendrites of a cell pick up signals of information from the closest neuron and process the information in the nucleus. After the message is processed, it continues down the neuron through the

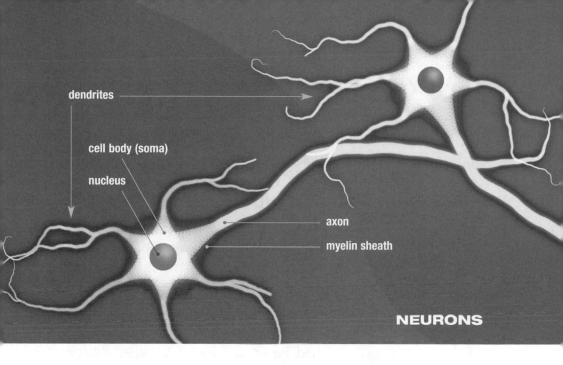

dendrites

cell body (soma)

nucleus

axon

myelin sheath

cell's **axon**, which is encased in a layer of fat known as **myelin**. When the information reaches the axon terminals, it is released into the open gap between neurons. This information (carried by neurotransmitters) travels across the gap reaching new dendrites of another cell, and the process begins all over again. So the information travels into the dendrites and out the axons from cell to cell, making its way from the brain to the body.

So when you decide to kick a soccer ball, your brain sends the message, which travels by neurotransmitters from neuron to neuron, for you to wind up your leg and kick the ball, all at lightening fast speed. You might want to take this thinking further, and explore what happens when someone damages their spinal cord, interfering with this brain messaging system.

Axon *the appendage of the neuron that transmits impulses away from the cell body*

Myelin *a white fatty material that forms a thick covering surrounding certain nerve fibers*

Help Your Brain Help You

A common misperception about the brain is that people are born with all of the neurons they'll ever have. Other common misperceptions include the idea that the brain stops growing at a certain age and that a person's capacity for learning is fixed. In almost every class you'll ever take, there will be a handful of students dubbed the "smart kids." Maybe you're identified with this label. Smart kids are recognized by their classmates as the students who ace every test, grasp new concepts before everyone else (or even know the material already), take advanced courses, etc. Perhaps you've looked at one of these learners, assumed he or she had a natural ability beyond your own, concluded there was nothing you could do about it, and resolved to maintain your own status quo rather than push yourself to level the playing field.

If this attitude sounds a lot like yours, re-read the common misperceptions listed above and re-think them so that you can see that they are exactly what we said—misperceptions. First, you are not born with all of the neurons you'll ever have. When neurons become damaged or degenerate, new ones develop. Second, your brain does not stop growing at a certain age. Your brain has endless potential for enlargement. The change in your brain size is not

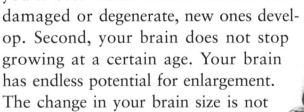

evident by a corresponding change in your head size, but it is manifested through new wrinkles and creases that form within the brain itself. In this way, the surface area of your brain can expand without becoming too large for your skull. Third, your capacity for learning is not fixed. As you may have gathered from the previous two points, you have the ability to create new neural pathways through regenerating neurons and the flexibility of your brain tissue. Each wrinkle and crease in your brain represents the birth of a new neural pathway, signaling your understanding of new concepts and mastery of new skills. Your brain always makes room to accommodate new facts.

The more you stimulate your brain by exposing it to new material and activities, the more connections form between neurons. In order to familiarize you with the basic structure of a neuron, you were presented earlier with a simplified version of how each nerve cell accepts messages from a neuron and passes this information onto other neurons. As the branching nature of dendrites indicates, however, signals do not pass from neuron to neuron in a strictly linear format. Interactions among neurons occur in every direction. The more your brain is prompted by new information and activity, the more neural pathways will establish intricate webs of communication with one another.

Think of a hobby that appeals to you, such as gardening. Starting your own garden could lead you to an interest in different types of bugs, and maybe you find butterflies particularly fascinating. Your attraction to butterflies may eventually inspire you to take up nature photography, which may lead to the study of different cameras with various optic apertures. Experimenting with fresh

Apertures *openings, as in holes, slits or gaps, that limit the amount of light entering through an optical instrument*

Collette was able to develop her passion for archeology by working one Saturday with the staff at the La Brea Tarpits. She is holding her raccoon skull.

pursuits and presenting your brain with new ideas gives it a chance to advance its current knowledge base and extend its network of neural pathways.

Keep It Fresh

The brain helps you learn a lot of things, but the knowledge you retain often results from the effort you put forth in the learning process. Practicing a skill or reviewing a concept assists information in moving from your short-term memory into your long-term memory. Think of playing an instrument. You may learn a new song on the piano, but if you don't look at a piano again for a month, chances are you'll forget the notes to the song. However, if you sit down and practice the music for twenty minutes each day for two weeks, you'll be much more likely to recall the song the next month. So you can see the value in studying and reviewing what you learn each day to help move the information into your long-term memory.

Similarly, if you study German in middle school and high school but never travel to Germany or use the language once you graduate, your brain will dismiss most of what you learned. The neural pathways responsible for your German language recall weaken as you get older, because your brain draws conclusions as to what information to keep and what to discard (through a process called synaptic pruning). By getting rid of un-accessed material, your brain makes room for absorbing more pertinent data. It's as they say, "Use it or lose it!"

Avoid Drug and Alcohol Use

Both your brain and body are negatively affected when you experiment with drugs and/or alcohol. As teens, your brains and bodies are still growing and changing, and alcohol and drugs can have profound effects. Alcohol slows the function of the nervous system (including the brain) and can block messages trying to get to the brain. It also affects your body, altering your perceptions, emotions, movement, vision and hearing. Early alcohol use can cause learning problems and lead to adult alcoholism. Bad habits relating to alcohol and drug use can form at any time of life, yet research shows that those who begin drinking by the age of fifteen are five times more likely to abuse or become dependent on alcohol than those who begin drinking after the age of twenty.

Experimenting with drugs or alcohol is a risk not worth taking (we'll talk more about taking positive risks in Chapter 8). For more information about the dangers of drugs and alcohol, review the resources in the appendix.

The Body

As you continue to grow over the next few years, you'll notice several physical changes that your body undergoes. For some of you, especially boys, these changes may not appear until you reach high school. Either way, now is still a good time to contemplate what lies ahead. Even if you begin your physical maturation later than your peers, you are still very much affected by the transformations going on in and around you.

Puberty comes at different times for different people. Genetics are involved, as well as your general health and body type. Girls who enter puberty in the later stages of grade school often feel embarrassed because they are the

first among their peers to physically mature. Similarly, boys who do not reach the start of puberty until middle or late high school can become self-conscious as they see their male classmates growing taller, getting deeper voices, shaving, and gaining muscle bulk.

Whether you fall into one of these two groups or are somewhere in the middle, try not to get discouraged. The physical changes you go through in middle school are challenging. Thankfully, puberty doesn't last forever!

Thinking to Myself

When my health teacher talks to my class about our changing bodies I feel so embarrassed I can't speak. I have a lot of questions but there's no way I can ask them aloud in class. I'm afraid everyone else already knows the answers. My older brothers tease me at home. They tell me things about what will start happening to me that I'm pretty sure aren't true. How can I tell the difference between what's true and what isn't? My teacher gave us some pamphlets about puberty that helped me understand, but mostly I wish I could just skip ahead a couple of years and leave it all behind me.

1.) Come up with three people this person could talk to regarding their concerns. Would it be difficult for you to ask these questions?

2.) Why do you think it is difficult to discuss puberty in our culture? What can be done to make such discussions easier and more comfortable?

Caring For Your Body

Listed below are some tips for taking care of your brain and body.

1. **Eat well.** Both your brain and body need optimal nutrition during these growing years. The more you can resist junk food, and choose fresh vegetables, fruits and lean meats, the better off you'll be. Many teens experience skin

Seeing Myself in Others

My name is Victoria. I love to be creative and enjoy decorating, painting, and making things look neat and fun. I hope to be an interior designer one day, and that's part of the reason why I'm involved in an international club called Odyssey of the Mind.

Odyssey groups are made up of five to seven teammates and are usually coached by parents. Each team is presented with five problems, and the group picks one problem. Adults are not allowed to give any suggestions. After picking a problem, it's time to brainstorm solutions. Teams are challenged to fulfill the requirements in an unusual and collaborative ways, which push our brains to think quickly and creatively.

Our last problem was called "Road Rally." My team constructed a car that used a drill for power, and we decorated it as Santa's sleigh with jingle bells and ornaments. We also built a device out of wood and metal blades that pushed balls down a ramp and shot them into the air for a snowball fight.

Creative thinking has really helped me in middle school with projects, especially in science. Science is my favorite subject because I love taking labs. In one lab, we were able to construct a volcano that actually exploded. I also created a science fair project on what type of toys dogs like best. I tested several different dogs and timed how long they played with each of three toys: a squeaky toy, a rubber ball, and a rubber chicken. The dogs played with the rubber chicken the longest.

I've used creative thinking in all kinds of situations. One of the best things about being a creative person is that I get to share my ideas with other people. That's what all of us need to do if we are to solve some of our world's biggest problems.

breakouts. Diet alone can't fix these problems, but eating fresh foods and drinking plenty of water, while avoiding greasy snacks, will help your cause. Discuss your diet with your doctor at your next check-up to ensure your eating will effectively support your growth and level of activity.

2. **Exercise.** It's important to devise an exercise routine that you'll stick to. If you play sports, your exercise routine will be built into your day. If not, see if you can ride your bike to school, take daily walks, or join a fitness class. You may begin to have weight or strength concerns during puberty. Exercising can improve your attitude about your looks as well as ensure that you stay healthy. Don't forget that plenty of exercise is important for the brain as well. Moving around increases the oxygen flow to the brain, helping the brain function better. It's been proven that students do better in mathematics if they receive their lessons after recess or gym. Research has also shown that senior citizens improve their memory and thinking by taking one long walk a day. So keep active—it will help your brain and body!

3. **Bathe regularly.** Until now, you may not have needed to take a shower or bath every day or even every two. But puberty can bring about more oil for the hair and skin. Taking the extra time to wash more often can help you feel better about your appearance. Many parents tend to back off mon-

itoring their middle school students' personal hygiene. But it can become a very important part of your social acceptance.

4. **Pay attention to pain.** Physical aches can be a natural part of growing up. But don't ignore your body. If they persist, it might be a warning that something is wrong. Always ask or tell someone if you experience pain of any kind, especially if it takes a while to go away.

5. **Get plenty of sleep.** If you are a typical teen or pre-teen, you live a busy life. Homework, activities, friends and family all compete for your time. Often, it's the sleep that falls by the way side. Studies now show that teenagers need as much, if not more sleep than toddlers. While you can't fit naps into your everyday life, try to develop a sleeping routine that gives you enough hours each night. While sleeping extra on the weekends feels good, you really can't make-up for the effect lost sleep has on your brain and body.

Seeking Help When You Need It

Taking proper care of the body and brain can be confusing at times for some teenagers. One of the most important things for you to learn is when and where to ask for help. For example, in an effort to eat a healthy diet, some teens might severely limit what and how much they eat. If this behavior becomes obsessive, it can lead to eating disorders that can harm the brain and body. If you come across this difficult situation, your best response is to talk with your parents and school counselor. Similarly, you might encounter other dangerous behaviors such as obsessive exercise, cutting or drug use. Your counselors are trained to help you navigate these difficult experiences and one of the smartest actions you can take in your life is to ask for help.

Define *neuron*.

_____

_____

_____

Use the word neuron in a sentence.

_____

_____

_____

_____

Define *dendrite*.

_____

_____

_____

Use the word dendrite in a sentence.

_____

_____

_____

_____

Define *axon*.

_____

_____

_____

Use the word axon in a sentence.

_____

_____

_____

Define *myelin*.

_____

_____

_____

Use the word myelin in a sentence.

_____

_____

_____

_____

_____

Define *apertures*.

_____

_____

_____

_____

Use the word apertures in a sentence.

_____

_____

_____

_____

_____

asking questions

List one thing you like about your appearance. List one thing you'd like to change.

_____

_____

How can you find a healthy balance between maintaining what you like and changing or accepting what you don't like?

_____

_____

_____

_____

What specifically can you do to stretch your brain's capacity?

_____

_____

_____

What can you do to make sure you retain the knowledge and skills you are currently developing?

_____

_____

_____

_____

What does this make you think of?
Journal about your thoughts.

Learning to
Take Risks

WHAT DO YOU NEED TO GROW?

can't sleep. I have a piano audition for a performing arts
school next week and I'm afraid I won't be accepted. What's
worse, the more nervous I get, the worse I usually play. But I
can't calm myself down. "It's very competitive, Kim," my mother says.
My dad questions if I should put so much energy into playing the

piano, and is trying to talk me out of auditioning. "The chances of ever becoming professional are slim, and even if you do," he says, "you'll never make any money." What if my parents are right? What if the school doesn't accept me? Even if it does, what then? Playing the piano has always been my greatest passion. I can't imagine my life without it. If I don't get accepted into the performing arts school, I'll feel like a failure. But if I don't even try, and just stick to my weekly lessons, I'm afraid I'll regret it later on down the road.

Have you ever felt like Kim? Have you ever wanted to try something, but let yourself be talked out of it by someone? Perhaps you've even talked yourself out of taking such a risk. Most people keep from trying new things because they fear failure. It is easier to stick with what you know how to do than risk looking foolish. But there is a cost.

Can you imagine if J.K. Rowling never finished her first **installment** of Harry Potter? A number of publishers rejected her manuscript, discouraging her from completing the book. She could have slipped her pages into a drawer and never finished. Instead, she continued to write. And that made all the difference. Now she is one of the most successful authors and exemplifies the rewards of taking a risk and persevering.

Installment *one of a number of parts*

Identifying Risks Worth Taking

What would you do if you weren't afraid of failing? It would be unfortunate if you never attempted your greatest dreams because a fear of coming up short stops you in your tracks. It's much easier to take the safe route, to do what is simply expected of you, and to resist pushing yourself beyond your comfort zone. But living this way can lead to an empty existence. Doing what you love to do or pursuing something that invigorates you can take a lot of courage, **dedication** and faith in yourself.

So, what are you afraid to do? Is there someone you'd like to make friends with but you don't know how to extend yourself? Would you like to join the speech team in middle school? Perhaps you have an aspiration like Kim's? Take a moment to list three things below that you'd like to attempt but might need a little extra encouragement to do so. Your list can include anything from asking a teacher for extra help to trying out for the school play.

Dedication *devotion to something*

Dedication, sacrifice and hard work allowed this student to receive a trophy for his baseball achievements.

1. _____

2. _____

3. _____

Now, look at your list. Go through each item and ask yourself what it would be like if you achieved the stated goal. What would you learn from the experience? What other experiences might result from trying this endeavor? What would be the worst thing that could happen if you weren't successful the first time you attempted this goal? What would you learn from trying?

Pursuing a goal offers several rewards, with only one being the actual accomplishment of what you set out to do. By taking a risk, trying your best, and keeping an open mind, regardless of the outcome, you'll learn things about yourself and others that will help you throughout your life.

Thinking to Myself

My parents and teachers keep telling me that I should get involved with an activity at school. I don't have many friends and am not very good at meeting people. Besides there is nothing I really want to do. I'd rather come home, sit on the couch and watch T.V. I wish they'd just leave me alone.

My older brother is good at everything he tries. It doesn't matter if it's tennis, theater or academics. He's the lucky one. Everything comes so easy for him.

1. Why do you think the parents and teachers encourage this student to get involved with something at school? How might it be of benefit?

2. If this was your friend, what kind of advice would you give?

Facing Your Fears

*C*onfronting what you are afraid of can be scary, and certainly can be unpleasant. But running from your fears and taking the easy way out has its own price. Ralph Waldo Emerson once said, "There are always two choices, two paths to take. One is easy. And the only reward is that it is easy." The same goes for your own life. You may escape the hardship or difficulties going after a dream may pose, but you miss out on so many potential rewards. This chapter opens with Kim's dilemma: she can audition for the performing arts school and try her best to pursue her music whole-heartedly, or continue taking weekly music lessons and avoid the angst of auditioning. Let's imagine the two different paths she might take.

Confront *to bring face-to-face*

Path One

Kim is terrified of the audition, which is just one week away. She stops practicing altogether because if she doesn't make it, it will be easier to blame it on lack of practice rather than admitting she tried her best but failed. A few days before the audition, she suddenly decides not to try out at all. She continues her weekly lessons but begins to spend more time shopping and watching TV. She misses being so passionate about piano, but tells herself that it is better this way. "Why pursue music now when it probably won't amount to much anyway?" she asks herself. Within a year, Kim gives up the piano all together.

Path Two

Kim is terrified of the audition, which is just one week away. She practices all week despite her fears she won't be accepted. The day of the audition she shakes uncontrollably, dizzy with nervousness, and her worst fear is realized. She doesn't get accepted to the school. At first she is very disappointed and a little embarrassed by her failure. But after a week she begins to see how much she learned by perfecting her piano program and preparing for such a challenge. The next month she's assigned a challenging project in science. All of her friends struggle to get the project done, but she breezes through it, realizing that the focus and dedication she applied preparing for her audition is really helping her now. She also knows the experience of auditioning this year will prepare her for the same piano audition next year. Kim continues to practice the piano with a hunch that things might turn out differently next year.

What did Kim gain by taking path one? What did she gain by taking path two? What are the costs to her for each decision? If Kim is an adult looking back on this experience, which path do you think she wished she took?

Putting yourself out there—through an audition, through volunteer work, through a new job or through learning an instrument for the first time—will help you learn what you are capable of achieving.

There is much to learn from taking risks. The two paths result in very different outcomes. When Kim follows her dream and auditions for the music school, her life does not become perfect. She is not selected to attend the school, but earns different rewards. The opposite path—not following her dream—proves to be safer, but much less rewarding. Which path would you take?

Nelson Mandela, a Nobel Peace Prize winner from South Africa, once said: "The greatest glory in life is not never failing, but rising every time we fall." The same can apply to your life. Just knowing you have the strength to stand up to your fears and take risks, no matter what the outcome, is cause for pride. It's surely a much better feeling than waking up 20 years from now and wondering what would have happened if you had done things differently.

Thinking to Myself

I've been forced to take risks and meet new friends. My family and I move a lot, and I just started at my fifth different school since kindergarten. I used to be afraid each time I started at a new school, but I'm learning to make friends more easily each time. I've found that if I get involved with a club or join a team, I usually can make some pretty good new friends within a few months. The advantage is that now I have friends who live all over the country. I hope that we can be in the same place again in the future. Maybe I'll even end up seeing some of them in college.

1. How do you think this student's attitude helps him/her with making new friends?

2. What would you do to initiate new friends if you were in this position? How can you apply this to making new friends in your life right now?

Finding Support

Deciding on a goal and stepping out of your comfort zone to pursue your interests are huge steps. Finding the right people to support your efforts can make all the difference. When looking for support, consider people who might provide encouragement, direction, insight, experience, and faith in you. It's important to surround yourself with the people who have your best interests in mind.

Seeing Myself in Others

My name is Ana. My dad was born and raised in Mexico, and my mom is American. I was born in the United States but spent most of my life in Mexico before moving back as a junior in high school. Living in two different countries has taught me that you have to take risks in order to discover yourself and learn about the world.

Stepping out of my comfort zone was essential to making friends in my new school. I was afraid people would reject me because everyone seemed to be on some kind of schedule with their lives already planned. I was used to being able to just drop in on people because the Mexican town I lived in was small and rural. Everyone knew everyone else. In America, I had to push myself to meet people in order to get involved.

My favorite sport has always been soccer, but my new school didn't have a team. I decided to try volleyball, but some of my teachers recommended cross country instead. They needed more girls on the team, and I figured it would keep me in shape for soccer.

I found that I loved running and was good at it. It was a way for me to find release and get rid of stress. Everything felt better after I ran. After joining cross country, I signed up for track. There was more of a personal challenge with cross country and track than with soccer. It's not just a competition against others; it's a competition against yourself and your own records.

Taking risks prepared me for the future. Even when I failed, there was something good to be learned. Failure made me more mature. If I hadn't tried new things, I would've regretted so many missed opportunities.

HOME AWAY FROM HOME by Ana Garcia

Why is this so hard? I've done this a million times again.
Nobody knows.
Not many show that it's a good thing to be my friend,
I usually step back,
And let things go by, but then I missed out on real fun times.
I'm tired of trying to make myself feel I'm at home.

Chorus:
I'm missing everything that always used to be.
But now that it's not here, I still want to be me.
I want to join this world, that's so different and new.
I want to be a girl who can smile but is still missing you.

I wanna take risks,
Make myself known. Should be used to being out of my
*   comfort zone.*
Make it OK.
Make it worthwhile. Make this a genuine smile.
I don't want out,
I actually want in; our life can be cool when it's changing.
Just tired of trying to make myself feel I'm at home.

Many students can find this type of support from their parents. If this is not the case for you however, look beyond your immediate family. Do you have a relative, a teacher, or a counselor who can help you achieve your goals? Perhaps you can seek help from a coach or mentor who **specializes** in the activity you are pursuing. Many adults appreciate being asked to share their expertise, so don't be afraid to ask them for their input.

As you identify key figures in your life that can provide you with much needed support, keep your eyes open for any detractors. People who are negative and cause you to seriously doubt yourself might be best avoided. When you are risking and putting yourself on the line, negative people can distract you from the task at hand. By remaining positive and surrounding yourself with positive people, you'll do a much better job of handling the challenges of risk taking.

Specialize *to pursue a specific activity, occupation, or field of study*

What you Gain

Taking a responsible risk on any level, whether pursuing a new activity or making friends with someone who appears different, can offer rewards. Each time you exit your comfort zone, you step into unfamiliar territory and this territory can feel scary, especially if you're not used to pushing yourself. However, you'll grow from the experience. Not only will you be closer to attaining the goal you set out to conquer, you will be stretched by the risk taking experience, helping you become a **well-rounded** person.

Well-rounded *to include many details or much variety*

One of the greatest benefits of taking responsible risks, however, is that your energy will be focused on a positive goal. Many students get into trouble when they are bored, they lack positive goals, and their energy isn't channeled into something productive. These are the times that students slip into negative risk taking—launching into activities that are dangerous and can cause serious problems. If you've worked hard to earn a starting spot on the soccer team, chances are you'll be less likely to make bad choices and take inappropriate risks which could cause you to lose all you've worked to earn. By identifying areas where you want to positively challenge yourself, making a commitment to these goals and finding the best support for you as possible, you'll keep your focus on things that will help you succeed in middle school.

WHAT HAVE YOU LEARNED?

Define *installment*.

_____

_____

_____

Write a sentence about your own life using the word installment.

_____

_____

_____

_____

Define *dedication*.

_____

_____

_____

Write a sentence about your own life using the word dedication.

_____

_____

_____

_____

Define *confront*.

_____

_____

_____

Write a sentence about your own life using the word confront.

_____

_____

_____

_____

Define *specialize*.

_____

_____

_____

Write a sentence about your own life using the word specialize.

_____

_____

_____

_____

Define *well-rounded*.

_____

_____

_____

Write a sentence about your own life using the word well-rounded.

_____

_____

_____

_____

asking questions

REFLECT AND RESPOND

What's a responsible risk that you've taken and succeeded with?

_____

_____

_____

_____

When did you take a risk that was not responsible?
What was the outcome?

_____

_____

_____

_____

Think back to a time when you experienced failure or
setback. How did you deal with it?

_____

_____

_____

_____

What would you change about the situation, your attitude,
or your response to the failure or setback?

_____

_____

_____

_____

What does this make you think of?
Journal about your thoughts.

The Mindset of Success

WHAT DOES YOUR ATTITUDE NEED TO BE?

As I run onto the football field to replace Howard, I can't help but think about how much bigger he is than me. All season I've tried to compensate for being a foot shorter and 50 pounds lighter than most of the guys. But now I must focus on Coach's words still ringing in my ears. "I'm giving you your shot, Vince," he said. "You've worked hard, so get out there and show me what you can do." I think about Howard, the player with the most field time and notoriety, and many of the others who laughed when I showed up at tryouts this season after being cut last year. But they started paying attention when they saw me running extra laps after practice and lifting weights in the weight room. Now it's my time. I take a deep breath and call the play. The center hikes me the ball, I take four steps back, see my connection and pass. The wide receiver leaps in the air, just feet from the end zone. No one's laughing now.

Howard was born with physical traits of a great athlete. However natural talent alone isn't everything. In fact, many coaches look just as hard at players who have the grit and determination, as they do players who possess natural gifts. What Vince lacked in physical attributes, he made up in determination. Remember that talent and determination together make up the equation for success.

When you play a card game, your ability to win only partially depends on the cards you are dealt. You still have to play. The act of winning ultimately comes down to how you manage the hand you are given. It is the same in life. Commonly, the personal limits you face make you work the hardest, and become strong. Learning how to work hard and apply yourself is everything. Without these limitations you might never know what you are capable of becoming.

If you want to make the most of what you're dealt in life, you need to acknowledge and develop your strengths while simultaneously working on areas that need improvement. As you approach these two challenges, adopting a positive outlook will significantly influence how your life unfolds.

Develop Optimism

ince worked hard to **compensate** for what his teammates viewed as inferiorities. These efforts ultimately led him to an accomplishment few people thought him capable of. Vince held strong to a belief that he could succeed—a mindset of success.

A mindset of success has several ingredients, but foremost among them is optimism. Whenever you catch yourself thinking you'll never be good at a particular subject because you struggle in class, push those thoughts away and replace them with more **constructive**

Compensate *to make up for something*

Constructive *to be helpful, useful, or beneficial*

A mindset of optimism will open all sorts of doors from the playing field to the classroom to the world of work.

ones. Instead of dwelling on where you've fallen short, create an action plan for how you can improve in the future. By developing an "I—can" attitude, and a plan for implementing this attitude, you can overcome your limitations and weaknesses.

It wasn't enough for Vince to want to be bigger, to possess more athletic ability. It wasn't even enough for him to "believe" he could be better and compete with those players who are taller and stronger. Vince had to marry his belief in himself with a plan of action: running extra laps and spending extra time in the weight room. He also had to know when to turn his mind off, disregarding negative thoughts reminding him how much smaller he was than the other players, and focus on the words of his coach, "You've worked hard, so get out there and show me what you can do."

Envision Your Success

Devoting your time to something that's meaningful to you requires dedication. Success from such dedication seldom arrives instantly. In fact, most achievements in life are reached through years of hard work, through **perseverance**. So how can you persevere? Especially when you experience failure? One hint is to envision your success.

Many Olympic gymnasts and divers practice this technique. They sit with their eyes closed and imagine they are executing a dive or trick. They go through each step in the process, landing the feat perfectly. Scientists have even learned that certain muscles in a person's body actually fire when

Perseverance *the will to keep working until a job is done despite difficulties*

they are envisioning such activities. Now of course their practice can't be limited to simply envisioning a dive or trick. They have to spend endless hours perfecting their efforts. But envisioning the perfect execution helps solidify the process in their mind and body.

Similarly, you can envision your success. Imagine your goal is to win the league championship on your cross country team. How will you feel when you accomplish your goal? How will you look? What will you say? What opportunities will open for you? Having a vision of yourself successful, and holding onto this vision when the going gets tough, will help you persevere. Just remember, you must get out there and do the work involved as well!

Thinking to Myself

My mom is only 15 years older than I am. I live in a small town with my grandparents where everyone knows everything about each others' lives. No one forgets anything about the past. Being raised here has been hard because most of the older people look at me and see the baby my 15-year-old parents were unable to care for by themselves. I think some of my teachers even see me this way. They don't mean to treat me differently, but they do. Next year I'll be in middle school, and it's located a few towns away. I can't wait to prove myself to people who don't know me and don't know my past. I've wanted to establish myself as my own person my whole life, and now I'll finally have a chance to thrive. I know I can do it.

1. What do you think success looks like to this person? What would it look like to you if you were in her shoes?

2. Why do you think it is hard for people to change the way they view this student? What does it say about how you want to be seen in the world?

Overcome Defeat

Vince was well aware of his physical disadvantage. He could have quit, especially after his teammates laughed at him. No one would have blamed him. But he didn't. He accepted the challenges he faced in spite of the possibility that he might be cut from the team a second time. Vince developed a plan of action. He followed through with the commitment he made to himself and he succeeded.

Failure or disappointment can be a powerful motivating force, if you channel it properly. The key is to use failure and setbacks to your advantage. Next time things don't turn out the way you hoped, ask yourself: "What worked well?", "What didn't work?", "How well was I prepared?", "How might have I prepared better?", "Where do I need to improve?", and "What can my opponents teach me?"

If you ask yourself these difficult questions and honestly **assess** your situation, you'll learn a lot about how to turn your failure into

Seeing Myself in Others

My name is Sean. My goal is to aim high in every area of my life and be 100% focused on whatever task is at hand.

I'm a member of multiple sports teams, including a traveling baseball team I've played on since I was 10. I hope to earn a scholarship to play sports in college, but that means I may have to narrow it down to one sport. It'll be a tough decision because what I decide to play will probably determine where I go to college. If I play basketball I might choose a big school in Tennessee or North Carolina. If I play football I might choose Florida, and baseball dominates in Arizona.

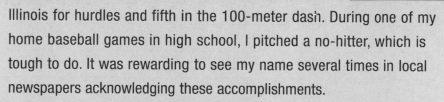

During my last year of middle school and my first year of high school, I was captain of my basketball team. I love to help people and see my teammates succeed. When I tried my hand at track for the first time in eighth grade, I took second in the state of Illinois for hurdles and fifth in the 100-meter dash. During one of my home baseball games in high school, I pitched a no-hitter, which is tough to do. It was rewarding to see my name several times in local newspapers acknowledging these accomplishments.

It hasn't all been an easy ride for me, though. Up until seventh grade, I had a real attitude problem. I didn't want anyone telling me what to do or giving me advice. Now I realize how constructive criticism actually helped me improve my skills and become a better person. People were just trying to help me, not put me down. I wanted to be successful, so I've worked hard and studied hard. You can build a foundation for success in high school by starting right where you are now.

success. You must however put this new information into action and try again. Learning from failure is good. Applying the lessons learned from failure is great. The more you remind yourself that failure and **adversity** don't necessarily mean defeat, and that perceived inabilities can be turned into extraordinary abilities, the more you develop a mindset of success.

You stand at a critical **threshold.** Being optimistic, envisioning the fulfillment of your goals and overcoming defeat make up the mindset of success—a framework for thinking that can help you achieve great things.

Assess *to evaluate*

Adversity *a state of hard times or trouble*

Threshold *a place or point of beginning or entering*

vocabulary

WHAT HAVE YOU LEARNED?

Define *compensate.*

_____

_____

_____

Write a sentence about your own life using the word compensate.

_____

_____

_____

_____

Define *constructive*.

_____

_____

_____

Write a sentence about your own life using the word constructive.

_____

_____

_____

_____

Define *perseverance*.

_____

_____

_____

Write a sentence about your own life using the word perseverance.

_____

_____

_____

_____

Define *adversity*.

_____

_____

_____

Write a sentence about your own life using the word adversity.

_____

_____

_____

Define *assess*.

_____

_____

_____

Write a sentence about your own life using the word assess.

_____

_____

_____

Define *threshold*.

_____

_____

_____

_____

Write a sentence about your own life using the word threshold.

_____

_____

_____

_____

asking questions

How positive is your current outlook on life? Explain.

_____

_____

_____

_____

What failure has contributed the most to where you
are now?

_____

_____

_____

_____

How could your mindset of success be improved?

_____

_____

_____

_____

What are your dreams and what can you do to reach them?

_____

_____

_____

_____

What does this make you think of?
Journal about your thoughts.

Books and Websites

Here are some useful resources on a variety of topics. The websites are alphabetized after their www prefixes and the books are alphabetized by author.

Academic Help

*I*t's natural to be better at some subjects than others, but there's always room for improvement in every class. The following resources can help you with your studies if you're struggling in a particular area. The sites can provide you with other useful tips you can use when approaching tests, group projects, paper assignments, and your everyday homework.

- Borden, Sarah. *Middle School: How to Deal.* Chronicle Books, LLC, 2005.—A girl's guide to the transition from elementary to middle school.

- www.brainmass.com—24/7 academic homework help. Pose a question and a qualified Online Teacher's Assistant (TA) or graduate student will provide a detailed explanation.

- **www.ed.gov**—U.S. Department of Education offers advice and links for homework help.

- **www.gatesfoundation.org/Pages/home.aspx**—The Bill and Melinda Gates Foundation provides research on national and global health and education issues affecting children and youth.

- Heard, Georgia. *Awakening the Heart: Exploring Poetry in Elementary and Middle School*. Heinemann, 1998. —A handbook that teaches tools for writing through the power of poetry.

- **homeworktips.about.com**—Find out your learning style or get study tips by subject and homework help with specific assignments.

- **www.ipl.org**—Internet Public Library provides homework help for teens.

- McKellar, Danica. *Math Doesn't Suck: How to Survive Middle-School Math Without Losing Your Mind or Breaking a Nail*. Penguin Group (USA), 2007.—Actress Danica McKellar has chosen to be a math role model in this guide for middle school students and their parents.

- Mosatche, Dr. Harriet S. *Too Old for This, Too Young for That! Your Survival Guide for the Middle School Years*. Free Spirit Publishing, Inc., 2000.—Includes quizzes, stories, surveys, and activities addressing common middle school issues.

- **www.proquestk12.com**—ProQuest is digital teaching and learning with lesson plans, test-taking tips, and homework help.

- **www.slco.lib.ut.us/kidhelp.htm**—A directory of web pages to help with homework, sorted by topic.

- **www.studygs.net**—Study Guides and Strategies provides an easy-to-use website on how to manage your time, study in groups, and resolve conflicts.

- Williams, Julie. *Smart Girl's Guide to Starting Middle School: Everything You Need to Know About Juggling More Homework, More Teachers, and More Friends!* American Girl Publishing, 2004.—A guide to starting middle school with confidence, including letters and advice from real students.

Health

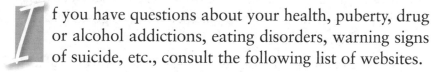f you have questions about your health, puberty, drug or alcohol addictions, eating disorders, warning signs of suicide, etc., consult the following list of websites.

- **www.aap.org**—the American Academy of Pediatrics offers current health information affecting children and teens.

- **www.al-anon.alateen.org**—Support group for friends and family members of alcoholics.

- **www.ama-assn.org**—the American Medical Association has the first health guides for children published by the AMA.

- **www.anred.com**—ANRED: Anorexia Nervosa and Related Eating Disorders offers information about eating disorders, including recovery and prevention.

- **www.child.net/drugalc.htm**—the National Children's Coalition provides facts on drugs and teen recovery groups.

- **www.childtrendsdatabank.org/index.cfm**—Child Trends Databank has the latest national trends and research on over 100 key indicators of child and youth well-being.

- **www.drugfree.org**—Partnership for a Drug-free America offers information about drugs, their effects, and personal accounts.

- Gruenwald Pfiefer, Kate. *American Medical Association Boy's Guide to Becoming a Teen.* Wiley, John & Sons,

Inc., 2006.—Get answers and advice to the most common health issues boys face during puberty.

- Gruenwald Pfiefer, Kate. *American Medical Association Girl's Guide to Becoming a Teen*. Wiley, John & Sons, Inc., 2006.—Get answers and advice to the most common health issues girls face during puberty.

- **www.madd.org**—Mothers Against Drunk Driving (MADD) provides victim services and education.

- **www.sadd.org**—Students Against Destructive Decisions (SADD) is students helping students make positive decisions about challenges in their daily lives.

- **www.save.org**—Suicide Awareness Voices of Education (SAVE) covers information on suicide prevention.

- **www.teenshealth.org/teen**—Provides information on your health, including drugs, fitness, and your changing body.

Learning Disabilities

*I*f you're having trouble keeping up with the rest of your class and are concerned that you might have a learning disability, the following links can provide you with more information.

- **www.apa.org**—American Psychological Association (APA) provides information on a variety of mental disorders.

- **www.autism-society.org**—Autism Society of America (ASA) provides support for families and friends within the autism spectrum.

- **www.chadd.org**—Children and Adults With Attention Deficit/Hyperactivity Disorder (CHADD) provides information and support for adults and children.

- **www.interdys.org**—International Dyslexia Association (IDA) is a non-profit organization promoting literacy through research and education.

- www.ldanatl.org—Learning Disabilities Association of America provides education resources for children and adults of normal or potentially normal intelligence.

- www.ldonline.com—LD Online: Learning Disabilities Information and Resources features an interactive site on resources for learning disabilities.

- www.nimh.nih.gov—National Institute of Mental Health (NIMH) offers information about symptoms and treatment of mental illnesses, and support to help those who have them.

Organizations and Extracurricular Activities

When you were in elementary school, your parents were probably the ones who signed you up for most of your extracurricular activities. Not only will there be more options available to you in middle school, but you'll most likely have a greater say in choosing where you want to get involved. The following websites can give you more information about organizations that might be of interest.

- www.afs.org—American Field Service (AFS) is an international nonprofit organization that offers cultural learning opportunities through intercultural exchange.

- www.bgca.org—Boys and Girls Clubs of America seek to motivate young people who may not otherwise have the means or resources to maximize their potential.

- www.yogakids.com—Learn about the benefits of yoga for both kids and adults and search for an instructor near you.

- www.girlscouts.org—Girl Scouts of America helps girls build characters and skills for success.

- **www.habitat.org**—Habitat for Humanity is a nonprofit organization that helps build affordable housing for those in need.

- **www.nasc.us/s_nasc/index.asp**—National Association of Student Councils promotes student leadership and provides information on activities, awards, and scholarships.

- **www.nhs.us/s_nhs/index.asp**—Offers information on the National Honor Society (for high school students) and the National Junior Honor Society (for middle school students), including activities and scholarships.

- **www.rotary.org**—Rotary International is made up of business leaders who promote community service and business ethics.

- **www.scouting.org**—Boy Scouts of America offers information on how to join cub scouting, boy scouting, and venturing and reports recent projects.

- **www.servenet.org**—Provides information on volunteering and community service.

- **www.sirc.ca**—Sports Information Resource Center offers information on nutrition, expert tips, and game play.

- **www.tai-chi.com**—T'ai chi Magazine

- **www.volunteermatch.org**—Volunteer Match helps you search for volunteer organizations in your area by entering your ZIP code or searching by name.

- **www.youthventure.org**—Youth Venture provides advice for young people seeking to develop their own small business ventures, community service organizations, or after-school clubs.

Understanding and Dealing with Problems

*D*uring your time in middle school, you may encounter any number of problems in your personal life that require attention. Follow the links below for more information on a variety of topics you might wish to learn more about or find applicable to your life.

- **www.adaa.org**—Anxiety Disorders Association of America (ADAA) offers prevention of anxiety disorders, including fears, phobias, and social anxiety.

- **www.adpoting.org**—Adopt: Assistance, Information, Support is an online community for people who have been adopted, families wanting to adopt, and family and friends of people who have been adopted.

- Blanco, Jodee. *Please Stop Laughing at Us....* Banbella Books, 2008.—Jodee uses her personal experience to provide advice, answers, and solutions for school bullying.

- **www.dbsalliance.org**—Depression and Bipolar Support Alliance educates patients, families, and friends of those with depression and other mental illnesses.

- **www.divorceonline.com**—Divorce Online offers information for those involved in divorce.

- Filitti, Jon. *Out of This World and Activity-Based Guidance Series for Kids.* YouthLight, Inc., 2005.—A comic book series of four on anger management and bullying.

- **www.friendsforsurvival.org**—Friends for Survival helps survivors of suicide loss.

- **www.girlshealth.gov**—GirlsHealth.gov was developed by the U.S. Office on Women's Health and offers information on relationships, fitness, and growing up.

- Goldman Koss, Amy. *The Girls*. Penguin Young Readers Group, 2002.—The fictional portrayal of a middle school clique.

- Kinney, Jeff. *Diary of a Wimpy Kid series*. Amulet Books, 2007.—An illustrated fictional series of four that follows the trials of a middle school boy.

- **www.knowgangs.com**—This site features gang related information and articles.

- Krulik, Nancy. *How I Survived Middle School series*. Scholastic, Inc., 2007.—A fictional series of seven books following the main character, Jenny McAfee, through her transition into and her experience through middle school.

- **www.mcgruff.org/Advice/gangs.php**—Learn about good friends vs. gangs, includes games and stories.

- **www.ncvc.org**—National Center for Victims of Crime provides resources to help victims of crime rebuild their lives.

- **www.nrscrisisline.org**—National Runaway Switchboard offers support and information for teens who are thinking about running away from home.

- **www.nsteens.org**—NSTeens provides advice for online safety, social networking, and cyber-bullying.

- **www.pflag.org**—Parents, Families, and Friends of Lesbians and Gays (PFLAG) provides information and support for friends and family members of gays and lesbians.

- **www.rainn.org**—The Rape, Abuse & Incest National Network provides information and crisis hotlines for victims.

- **www.safe-alternatives.com/index.html**—SAFE-Alternatives provides information and resources for ending self-abuse.

- **www.safeyouth.org**—National Youth Violence Prevention Resource Center (NYVPRC) provides information on prevention of violence and bullying.

- www.shopliftingprevention.org—National Association for Shoplifting Prevention provides support services and programs for people who struggle with shoplifting.

- www.starbright.org—the Starbright Foundation offers an online network where hospitalized children and teens can interact with each other and build a community of peers and support.

- www.stepfamilies.info/about.php—The National Stepfamily Resource Center is committed to providing resources for children who are members of stepfamilies.

- www.stopcyberbullying.org—This site offers tips for dealing with cyber-bullying.

- www.stophazing.org—StopHazing.org offers information on hazing for students.

- www.teenangels.com—Teen Angels posts stories of cyber bullying victims and explains what they went through and how they overcame their problems.

- www.teenwire.com—this Planned Parenthood Federation of America website offers information on relationships and sexual health for teens.

- www.violencepreventioninstitute.com—This site offers information regarding gang membership and gang behavior.

- Willard, Nancy. *Cyberbullying and Cyberthreats*. Research Pr Pub, 2007.—Provides information for parents, teachers, counselors, and administrators on how to prevent and respond to cyberbullying.

Note: several of these resources were found as links on the following website:

- http://www.kidshealth.org/teen

other success books by carol carter

The following books are available through Prentice Hall Publishers.
Visit www.prenhall.com (search by keywords "keys to").

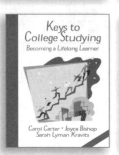
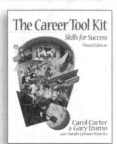

The following books are available through LifeBound. Visit www.lifebound.com.

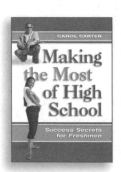
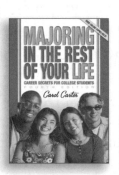

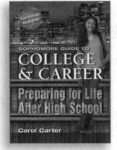
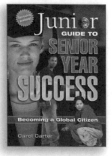